An American Bounty

An American Bounty

PHOTOGRAPHY BY LOUIS WALLACH

RIZZOLI
NEW YORK

To all of the individuals who have contributed to this book in ways large and small, we extend our heartfelt appreciation. We would especially like to recognize those who created and developed the recipes that appear in this book: Ferdinand Metz, Tim Ryan, Jim Heywood, Paul Sartory, Dave Megenis, Tim Rodgers, Jonathan Zearfoss, Greg Zifchak, Tom Peer, Tom Kief, Phil Delaplane, Markus Färbinger, Kathy Shepard, Liz Briggs. Thanks also to Terry Finlayson and Randi Foreman.

We would also like to thank our editor at Rizzoli, Carole Lalli, her assistant, Liz Keyser, the designer, Joel Avirom, and the photographer Louis Wallach for his wonderful work.

PHOTOS

FACING CONTENTS PAGE: Pan-fried Ham Steak with Red-eye Gravy
CONTENTS PAGE: top, Mushroom Barley Soup; *bottom,* American Bounty Fudge Cake

First published in the United States of America in 1995 by
Rizzoli International Publications, Inc.
300 Park Avenue South, New York, New York 10010

Copyright © 1995 Rizzoli International Publications, Inc.

Library of Congress Cataloging-in-Publication Data
An American Bounty : great contemporary cooking from the Culinary
    Institute of America.
        p.   cm.
    Includes index.
    ISBN 0-8478-1908-6
    1. Cookery, American.   I. Culinary Institute of America.
TX715.A5115 1995
641.5973—dc20   95-16918
                                                               CIP

DESIGNED BY JOEL AVIROM

DESIGN ASSISTANT: JASON SNYDER

Printed and bound in Singapore

*F*or nearly twenty years—more than half my life—American food has been my personal and professional focus. The pursuit of the freshest and finest products of the American harvest has led me to a discovery of the wealth and diversity of regional food and, most important, to the roots of our culinary heritage. To reap the benefits of one is to reap the benefits of the other. Over the past few decades many chefs, writers, and teachers across America have helped raise an awareness of and instill pride in this heritage and by so doing have created the new, vital image of American cuisine today. Much has been accomplished.

When the Culinary Institute opened the doors of The American Bounty Restaurant back in 1982, it again affirmed the Institute's leadership role. The restaurant has been a showcase for regional foods and preparations from all over America; it has contributed to the American Food Movement in a very special way. By educating its students in the ways of American food, it has trained present and future generations of American cooks and chefs. And now, the Institute will reach so many more through the collection of recipes found in this book.

I can remember, as if it were only yesterday, the first time I entered The American Bounty. I was amazed by the array of wonderful warm breads and biscuits, the cleverness of serving a trio of different soups and chowders, and the uniqueness of listing regional favorites as menu entrées. The baked-to-order fresh fruit cobblers seem special to this day.

The history, heritage, culinary hints, and recipes found in this wonderful book will do as much to nourish other enthusiasts of American cookery, whether novices or experts.

Larry Forgione
Chef and Restaurateur

Contents

INTRODUCTION

We first opened the doors of The American Bounty, one of four public restaurants at The Culinary Institute of America, in August 1982. At the time, magazine and newspaper articles, forums, and symposiums were celebrating the emergence of a national "cuisine." At the same time they tried to define what that might mean. We knew intuitively that there was something special about the way foods were prepared and served in this country. And, in devising the philosophy for our newest restaurant, we tried to capture the sense of excitement and direction we all were feeling.

Far from attempting to produce the ultimate credo for an American cuisine, The American Bounty had and still has as its mission the rediscovery of recipes, foods, and traditions that spoke to the heart of what Americans across the country were enjoying in their homes. The dishes that appeared on the first American Bounty menu spanned the regions of this country: New England Shore Dinner, New Orleans-style Gumbo, Pennsylvania Dutch Chicken Soup. We selected from among the wines and beers produced domestically. Today, we are confident that our commitment to learning about American cooking has helped to open doors for both our students and our guests.

American cooking embraces a diversity that runs the gamut from the traditional dishes of Great Britain and Western Europe to those brought from African, Caribbean, Asian, and Middle Eastern nations. The give and take between the New World and the Old has blurred any distinct lines that might once have made a definition easy. The United States certainly is not unique in this regard, however. The history of cooking and cuisine for any society is one of travel, conquest, experimentation, exploration—much like the histories of art, fashion, commerce, and information. What appears to make a dish American is something altogether different from what any single recipe, ingredient, region, or cultural subset can encompass. Nor is it simply a hodgepodge of foods, prepared and served with a sense of freedom and abandon that recognizes no boundaries. A succinct definition of what constitutes an American cuisine is perhaps no less elusive now than it was more than a decade ago.

American cooking is a vital, generous, and open-handed approach to foods and dining. There is a sense of robustness, energy, focus, and a celebration of what is special about a region, a food, or a tradition. At the restaurant, our most recent menus feature foods that fit relatively few stereotypes. We serve gnocchi, stir-frys, pot stickers, enchiladas, and risottos. These dishes might appear, on the surface, to have strayed from what was once considered true about American cuisine.

The approach we now take is more free-wheeling, and less dogmatic, than might have been permissible early on, as we first examined what yardsticks existed to measure American cooking. The constant rediscovery of native and heirloom ingredients and dishes, an increased appreciation of the historical events and influences that have shaped our country and the foods we eat, and a growing pride in regional specialties have all made a mark on the ever-evolving landscape of American cuisine.

The recipes featured in this book have been developed and served in The American Bounty Restaurant as well as in other classrooms and kitchens throughout the school. Regional dishes, from not only the Hudson Valley area, where The Culinary Institute of America is located, but also such areas as the Midwest, Southwest, the Pacific Coast, the South, Mid-Atlantic, and New England, all can be found. They may be faithful renderings of familiar dishes. Or they may be new creations, inspired by regional influences and ingredients. Whatever the case, they are prepared with careful attention to sound basic culinary practices.

Accepting diversity, celebrating the richness of our many cultural influences, and enjoying what is best about all that we have around us is itself at the heart of what is American. We can all take pride in the rich heritage that makes this country what it is and we invite you to join us at our national table, to share in a feast of the foods that have established An American Bounty.

Tim Ryan
Senior Vice President,
The Culinary Institute of America

Introduction

Appetizers & Salads

B.L.T. Salad with Buttermilk-Chive Dressing

*T*his salad reinterprets the classic "bacon, lettuce, and tomato" sandwich, one of the most popular lunch offerings in any diner or café. Alternate slices of red and yellow tomatoes for extra visual appeal.

MAKES 4 SERVINGS

12	bacon strips
2	whole-wheat rolls, cubed
2	tablespoons olive oil
3	garlic cloves, minced
½	teaspoon salt
¼	teaspoon freshly ground black pepper, or to taste
1	head Boston lettuce, separated into leaves, rinsed, and dried
2	large tomatoes, sliced ½ inch thick
¾	cup Buttermilk-Chive Dressing (recipe follows)

1. Preheat the oven to 400 degrees F. Lay the bacon strips on a baking sheet, and bake them in the oven for about 8 minutes, or until brown and crisp. Transfer the bacon to a plate lined with paper towels.

2. Toss the cubed whole-wheat rolls, olive oil, garlic, salt, and pepper together in a baking dish and toast in the oven for 8 to 10 minutes.

3. Arrange the lettuce in a salad bowl or on individual plates. Top with the sliced tomatoes, bacon strips, and croutons.

4. Drizzle the dressing over the salad and serve at once.

NUTRITION INFORMATION, PER SERVING, WITH 3 TABLESPOONS BUTTERMILK-CHIVE DRESSING: 365 calories, 10 grams protein, 27 grams fat, 21 grams carbohydrates, 830 milligrams sodium, 22 milligrams cholesterol.

AHEAD OF TIME: The croutons can be prepared in advance. However, the salad is most successful when the bacon is cooked just before the salad is served.

Preceding Page:
Soft Shell Crabs
with Pecans, Dill,
and Grapefruit

BUTTERMILK-CHIVE DRESSING

MAKES ¾ CUP

⅓ cup buttermilk	½ teaspoon freshly squeezed lemon juice
¼ cup prepared mayonnaise	¼ teaspoon Old Bay seasoning
2 tablespoons corn oil	(optional)
2 tablespoons minced fresh chives	Dash of Worcestershire sauce
1 tablespoon red wine vinegar	Salt to taste.
Dash of Tabasco or similar	Freshly ground black pepper
hot pepper sauce	to taste

1. Stir or shake all the ingredients in a bowl or jar to blend well.

2. Adjust the seasoning to taste by adding more salt, pepper, lemon juice, Worcestershire, or chives. Store in the refrigerator.

NUTRITION INFORMATION, PER SERVING (3 TABLESPOONS): 100 calories, trace of protein, 10 grams fat, trace of carbohydrates, 60 milligrams sodium, 5 milligrams cholesterol.

PREPARATION NOTES: This dressing will stay fresh for up to 4 days in the refrigerator. Be sure to stir or shake well before serving. It is best to allow the dressing 2 to 3 hours to fully develop its flavor before serving.

SERVING SUGGESTIONS: This dressing is equally good in a potato salad or as a dip for crudité. It also is an excellent topping for baked potatoes and a good dressing for chicken salad or a simple mixed green salad.

CHILLED STEAK AND BARLEY SALAD

This is a great salad for the day after an outdoor summer barbecue. Grilled pork, seafood, chicken, or vegetables are equally compatible with the sweet nutty flavor of barley.

MAKES 4 SERVINGS

⅔	cup pearl barley
¾	teaspoon salt, or to taste
1	tomato, diced
1	cucumber, peeled, seeded, and diced
1	cup sliced raw mushrooms
2	tablespoons finely diced sun-dried tomatoes, reconstituted (page 191)
¾	cup extra-virgin olive oil
¼	cup white wine vinegar
2	tablespoons chopped fresh tarragon leaves
¼	teaspoon freshly ground black pepper
1	bunch arugula, stems removed and rinsed
8 to 12	thin slices grilled steak

1. Bring 2 cups of water to a rolling boil. Add the barley and ½ teaspoon of the salt. Reduce the heat to a simmer and cook, covered, over low heat for 40 to 45 minutes, or until the barley is tender; drain thoroughly, then spread the barley in a thin layer to cool quickly.

2. Combine the barley, tomato, cucumber, mushrooms, and sun-dried tomatoes in a bowl.

3. Whisk together the oil, vinegar, tarragon, remaining ¼ teaspoon salt, and pepper. Pour the vinaigrette over the barley mixture and toss to coat evenly.

4. Mound the arugula on a chilled platter or individual plates and top with the barley salad. Arrange the steak slices over the salad.

NUTRITION INFORMATION, PER SERVING: 629 calories, 22 grams protein, 23 grams fat, 36 grams carbohydrates, 315 milligrams sodium, 52 milligrams cholesterol.

AHEAD OF TIME: The barley can be cooked and dressed up to a day in advance. Mix the cooked barley with the vinaigrette while it is still warm, cool to room temperature, cover tightly, and refrigerate. Let the barley mixture return to room temperature before serving.

SERVING SUGGESTIONS: This is a substantial main-course salad; drink a rich amber ale or lager with it and follow with Shaker Lemon Pie (page 178).

COLESLAW

*R*eputations have been made on the basis of this humble salad of shredded cabbage with a creamy dressing. The name originates from the Dutch *koolsla*, or cabbage *(kool)* and salad *(sla)*. Cookbooks from the early 1900s often specify boiled dressings which could keep the slaw fresh, under refrigeration, for several days or even as long as a week.

Today, sweet, cooked dressings are still preferred in some parts of the country. This recipe calls for less sugar than some, and is prepared by simply stirring together mayonnaise, sour cream, and seasonings.

MAKES 6 SERVINGS

⅔	cup sour cream	1	teaspoon celery seeds
¼	cup prepared mayonnaise	¼	teaspoon salt, or to taste
¼	cup cider vinegar	¼	teaspoon freshly ground black pepper
½	tablespoon dry mustard	3	cups shredded green cabbage
2	tablespoons sugar	½	cup shredded carrots

1. Mix the sour cream, mayonnaise, vinegar, mustard, sugar, and celery seeds together in a large bowl until smooth. Add the salt and pepper.

2. Add the cabbage and carrots, and toss to coat evenly.

NUTRITION INFORMATION, PER SERVING (½ CUP): 87 calories, 1 gram protein, 6 grams fat, 8 grams carbohydrates, 128 milligrams sodium, 8 milligrams cholesterol.

VARIATIONS: Fruit- or herb-flavored vinegars can be substituted for the cider vinegar. Use a combination of cabbages (Savoy, red, bok choy, or white) to create a multicolored version. Include other shredded vegetables such as celery, red or green peppers, or jícama. Scatter poppy seeds over the coleslaw.

LOWER-FAT VERSION: Use a reduced-fat sour cream, or substitute low- or nonfat yogurt for part or all of the sour cream. Use a reduced-fat version of mayonnaise, or try one of the tofu-based dressings.

Citrus Slaw with Avocado and Red Onion

*T*his vegetable salad has brilliant colors and a taste to match. The grapefruit vinaigrette adds a definite blast of flavor.

Makes 4 servings

1 cup fresh spinach leaves, washed thoroughly, stems removed, and finely shredded	¾ cup Grapefruit Vinaigrette (page 15)
1 cup finely shredded red cabbage	1 avocado
1 cup finely shredded Savoy cabbage	1 grapefruit, peeled and cut into segments
½ cup julienned red onion	½ teaspoon cracked black peppercorns

1. Toss together the spinach, cabbages, red onion, and ½ cup of the vinaigrette in a salad bowl.

2. Peel, pit, and cut the avocado lengthwise into slices; toss gently with the remaining vinaigrette until evenly coated.

3. Arrange the avocado and grapefruit on top of the cabbage mixture and top with the cracked peppercorns.

Nutrition information, per serving: 280 calories, 4 grams protein, 24 grams fat, 20 grams carbohydrates, 25 milligrams sodium, 0 milligrams cholesterol.

Preparation Notes: To peel and divide a grapefruit into segments, first slice away the top and bottom ends. Place on a cutting board on end and slice the rind away, removing all traces of pith. Cut the individual segments away from the connecting membranes, so that only the meat remains.

Serving Suggestions: This slaw is a fine complement for grilled or pan-roasted fish or for Mustard-Fried Chicken (page 87).

CAESAR SALAD

*C*ulinary lore has it that this salad was created by Caesar Cardini in 1924 at his restaurant in Tijuana, Mexico.

MAKES 4 SERVINGS

2 garlic cloves, peeled and cut in half	1 head romaine lettuce, leaves rinsed and torn into pieces
1/3 cup extra-virgin olive oil	
3 tablespoons fresh lemon juice	1/2 teaspoon salt, or to taste
1 whole egg (optional)	1/2 teaspoon freshly ground black pepper, or to taste
2 anchovy fillets, mashed into a paste	
4 tablespoons grated Parmesan cheese	1/2 cup garlic-flavored or plain croutons

1. Rub the inside of a large wooden salad bowl with the split garlic cloves, pressing firmly against the bowl.

2. Add the oil, lemon juice, egg, and anchovies to the bowl, and blend well with a fork until the dressing thickens.

3. Add the lettuce and toss until it is evenly coated with the dressing.

4. Add the Parmesan and salt and pepper, and top with croutons.

NUTRITION INFORMATION, PER SERVING: 236 calories, 6 grams protein, 21 grams fat, 6 grams carbohydrates, 500 milligrams sodium, 60 milligrams cholesterol.

PREPARATION NOTES: A whole egg, coddled or raw, is traditional in a Caesar dressing. To coddle an egg, place it in a pan of simmering water. Cover the pan and remove it from the heat. The egg is properly coddled after 2 minutes. Crack and use as above.

VARIATION: For a special presentation, use only the tender leaves from the heart of the romaine lettuce, and leave them whole, rather than tearing them into pieces.

Two tablespoons of pasteurized or frozen egg product can be substituted for the raw whole egg.

SERVING SUGGESTIONS: Garnish with curls of the best Parmesan you can find.

WARM BLACK-EYED PEA SALAD

This versatile salad proves that black-eyed peas are not just for New Year's Eve. The lemon zest and fresh basil add a refreshing tang, which provides lightness in a dish you might expect to be heavier.

MAKES 4 SERVINGS

⅓ cup extra-virgin olive oil	1 sprig of fresh rosemary
⅓ cup minced onion	1 sprig of fresh thyme
4 teaspoons minced garlic	1 bay leaf
Juice and zest of 1 lemon	2 tablespoons chopped fresh basil leaves
¾ cup dried black-eyed peas	½ teaspoon salt, or to taste
3 cups chicken (page 193) or vegetable broth (page 192) or water	¼ teaspoon freshly ground black pepper, or to taste

1. Heat 1 tablespoon of the oil in a heavy saucepan over high heat. Add the onion, about 3 teaspoons of garlic, and the lemon zest, and sauté lightly, just until the mixture releases its aroma, about 3 minutes.

2. Add the peas, broth, rosemary, thyme, and bay leaf, and bring to a boil. Reduce the heat to low and simmer until the peas are thoroughly tender, about ½ hour. Add water if necessary to keep the peas covered.

3. Combine the remaining oil and garlic, lemon juice, and basil in a serving bowl.

4. Remove the rosemary, thyme, and bay leaf from the peas; drain and add to the lemon-basil vinaigrette. Toss the peas gently until evenly coated with the dressing. Season to taste with salt and pepper.

5. Serve warm or at room temperature.

NUTRITION INFORMATION, PER SERVING: 234 calories, 4 grams protein, 20 grams fat, 10 grams carbohydrates, 335 milligrams sodium, 5 milligrams cholesterol.

PREPARATION NOTE: The peas should remain whole, yet be tender, so avoid cooking them to mush or breaking them by stirring them excessively as they cook.

Romaine and Apple Salad with Maytag Blue Cheese, Walnuts, and Port Wine Vinaigrette

This is a particularly successful combination of flavors and textures. Blue-veined cheeses, nuts, and port wine is a classic ending to a meal, so you might want to serve this after a main course, but it would be an excellent opener as well.

MAKES 6 SERVINGS

1 head romaine lettuce, torn into pieces, rinsed, and dried

1 bunch watercress, trimmed, rinsed, drained, and dried

½ cup Port Wine Vinaigrette (page 15)

1 Golden Delicious apple, cored and thinly sliced

1 Red Delicious apple, cored and thinly sliced

½ cup toasted walnut halves (page 192)

½ cup crumbled Maytag blue cheese

1. Combine the romaine lettuce and watercress in a salad bowl.
2. Add the Port Wine Vinaigrette and toss to coat lightly.
3. Scatter the sliced apples, walnuts, and blue cheese over the lettuce and serve.

NUTRITION INFORMATION, PER SERVING: 365 calories, 6 grams protein, 30 grams fat, 20 grams carbohydrates, 345 milligrams sodium, 10 milligrams cholesterol.

VARIATIONS: A combination of greens with assertive flavors, such as endive, escarole, chicory, oak leaf, or raddichio, are good alternatives to the romaine.

Other blue-veined cheeses, such as Gorgonzola or Roquefort, can replace Maytag blue cheese.

CRAB CAKES

Crab cakes can be found all around the country, but they truly belong to the Chesapeake Bay area. There are many versions—"Baltimore" crab cakes, for instance, simply are made from crab meat blended with mayonnaise, dipped in flour and beaten egg, and pan-fried. This more elaborate version has a rich, seafood flavor and a fine texture.

MAKES 4 SERVINGS, 3 CRAB CAKES PER SERVING

14	ounces fresh lump crab meat		1	tablespoon chopped fresh chives
2	ounces scallops, roughly cut up if large		½	teaspoon celery salt
2	tablespoons prepared mayonnaise		¼	teaspoon ground white pepper
1	tablespoon heavy cream		1	cup dry bread crumbs
2	eggs		½	cup vegetable oil, or as needed
⅓	cup fresh bread crumbs			for frying

1. Carefully pick over the crab meat, removing any bits of cartilage or shell.
2. Purée the scallops in a blender until smooth.
3. Combine the scallop purée with the mayonnaise, cream, and 1 egg in a large bowl and stir until smooth.
4. Mix in the fresh bread crumbs, chives, celery salt, and white pepper; fold in the crab meat.
5. Divide the mixture into 12 oval cakes about ½ inch thick.
6. Dip the crab cakes in the dry bread crumbs, pressing them gently but evenly over the top, bottom, and sides of each cake.
7. Heat ¼ inch of vegetable oil in a skillet over medium heat until almost smoking.
8. Sauté the crab cakes for 2 to 4 minutes on each side, or until golden brown. Serve hot.

NUTRITION INFORMATION, PER CAKE: 517 calories, 31 grams protein, 31 grams fat, 29 grams carbohydrates, 800 milligrams sodium, 225 milligrams cholesterol.

PREPARATION NOTES: The crab cakes can be prepared in advance, then held, uncovered, in the refrigerator, for up to 1 hour before cooking, which turns out beautifully crisp cakes.

SERVING SUGGESTIONS: Serve as a first course or make mini-crab cakes and serve them with cocktail or tartar sauce with cocktails.

Basic Vinaigrette and Variations

There are a number of variations possible using this basic recipe. Besides the specific vinaigrettes that follow, feel free to experiment with different oils and vinegars or other acidic ingredients to create dressings. Balsamic, sherry, or port vinegars used in moderation are better choices than red or white wine vinegars if wine is to be served with the salad course.

MAKES ABOUT 1 CUP, OR ENOUGH FOR 12 SERVINGS

¾	cup vegetable oil	2	tablespoons chopped fresh herbs such
¼	cup red wine vinegar		as chives, parsley, tarragon, chervil,
½	teaspoon dry mustard		basil, dill, or others (optional)
½	teaspoon salt, or to taste		
¼	teaspoon freshly ground black pepper, or to taste		

Whisk or shake all the ingredients together in a small bowl or jar. Shake or whisk the vinaigrette again before using if it has stood for more than a few minutes.

NUTRITION INFORMATION, PER SERVING (1½ TABLESPOONS): 150 calories, trace of protein, 16 grams fat, 2 grams carbohydrates, 145 milligrams sodium, 0 milligrams cholesterol.

PREPARATION NOTES: Store under refrigeration if the vinaigrette is not needed immediately. Allow it to return to room temperature before using.

VARIATIONS:

BALSAMIC VINAIGRETTE: Use extra-virgin olive oil for all or part of the vegetable oil, replace half the red wine vinegar with balsamic vinegar, and add some lightly sautéed shallots or garlic.

MUSTARD AND ROASTED GARLIC VINAIGRETTE: Add 2 tablespoons of mustard (Dijon-style, Pommery, herb-flavored, coarse-grain, or a combination) and 2 to 3 cloves of roasted garlic that have been mashed to a paste.

SHERRY VINAIGRETTE: Replace all or half of the vegetable oil with a nut oil such as hazelnut, walnut, or almond. Use sherry vinegar to replace the red wine vinegar.

GRAPEFRUIT VINAIGRETTE: Use peanut or safflower oil to replace the vegetable oil, add a few drops of dark sesame oil, use grapefruit juice to replace the vinegar, and add a few drops of soy or tamari sauce. Add a teaspoon of brown sugar, maple syrup, or honey to smooth out the flavor, if desired.

PORT WINE VINAIGRETTE: Use a combination of walnut and olive oil to replace the vegetable oil. Use equal parts of port wine and cider vinegar to replace the red wine vinegar.

SERVING SUGGESTIONS: Apart from their use to dress salads, these vinaigrettes can be used as marinades for grilled poultry, fish, or vegetables. Drizzle over steamed vegetables, or toss into cold cooked grains or pastas.

TURKEY COBB SALAD

*T*his is a version of the Cobb Salad made enormously famous at the Brown Derby restaurant, Hollywood's favorite hangout during its golden age. The original was made with chicken by the Derby's owner, Bob Cobb, on a late-night raid for a snack.

4 SERVINGS

4 bacon slices, diced	1 head romaine lettuce, torn into shreds
6 tablespoons vegetable oil	1 cup cubed, boneless, skinless turkey
2 tablespoons cider vinegar	breast
1 tablespoon fresh lemon juice	1 avocado, peeled, pitted, and diced
1 tablespoon Dijon-style mustard	1 stalk celery, sliced on the bias
2 tablespoons chopped fresh parsley	2 scallions, sliced on the bias
Salt and freshly ground pepper to taste	4 ounces blue cheese, crumbled (½ cup)

1. Cook the bacon until crisp in a heavy skillet over medium-high heat. Remove the bacon and drain it on paper towels. When the bacon is no longer hot, crumble it.

2. Blend the oil, vinegar, lemon juice, mustard, parsley, salt, and pepper thoroughly in a large mixing bowl.

3. Add the lettuce and toss to combine. Lift the lettuce out of the bowl onto a platter or individual plates, allowing any excess dressing to drain back into the bowl.

4. Arrange the turkey, avocado, celery, and scallions over the lettuce. Drizzle the remaining dressing over the salad. Top with crumbled blue cheese and bacon. Serve at once.

NUTRITION INFORMATION, PER SERVING: 485 calories, 14 grams protein, 45 grams fat, 7 grams carbohydrates, 475 milligrams sodium, 40 milligrams cholesterol.

VARIATIONS: Use chicken to replace the turkey. Or, eliminate the meat altogether. Blue cheese is traditional but cubed Monterey Jack, feta, or goat cheese is good, too.

SERVING SUGGESTIONS: Make 1 large platter for a buffet or smaller individual plates. Fresh, sparkling wines make a good beverage choice. Add a loaf of crusty sourdough bread.

AVOCADO WITH
MARINATED FIDDLEHEAD FERNS

*F*iddlehead" refers to ferns at the stage in their life cycle when the tightly coiled tip (known as a crosier) has just emerged from the soil. Ostrich ferns are raised for the commercial harvest of their edible fiddle-shaped heads. Available from April to early July, fiddleheads should be a clear jade green, firm, and no more than approximately one inch in diameter.

MAKES 4 SERVINGS

½	pound fiddlehead ferns		¼	teaspoon salt, or to taste
2	tablespoons balsamic vinegar		¼	teaspoon freshly ground black pepper, or to taste
1	teaspoon chopped fresh thyme leaves, or ½ teaspoon dried		¼	cup extra virgin olive oil
1	garlic clove, minced		2	ripe avocados
2	teaspoons Dijon mustard			

1. Trim away any woody stem ends from the fiddleheads. Bring a pot of water to a rapid boil and blanch the fiddleheads until soft, 3 to 4 minutes. Drain thoroughly.

2. Place the vinegar, thyme, garlic, mustard, salt, and pepper in a bowl. Add the oil gradually, whisking until thoroughly blended.

3. Drain the fiddleheads and add them to the marinade at once; marinate for several hours or overnight.

4. Slice the avocados in half just before serving. Remove the pit and peel away the skin.

5. Arrange the avocado halves on a serving platter or on individual plates. Place the marinated fiddleheads in the hollow of each avocado half and drizzle with any vinaigrette remaining in the bowl.

NUTRITION INFORMATION, PER SERVING: 300 calories, 4 grams protein, 29 grams fat, 11 grams carbohydrates, 111 milligrams sodium, 0 milligrams cholesterol.

PREPARATION NOTES: The success of this dish depends upon the quality of the avocados. To test an avocado for ripeness, cradle it in the palm of your hand and gently close your fingers around it; it should barely yield. If necessary, let the fruit ripen for a day or two in an earthenware bowl or a brown paper bag at room temperature.

VARIATION: Fresh asparagus are a good substitute for the fiddleheads, and grilled Vidalia onions would be a nice addition to the plate.

SERVING SUGGESTIONS: This is a perfect first course for a springtime meal. A main course of shad roe, salmon, or halibut would follow well.

Grilled Tuna Salad with Jícama, Artichokes, and Peppers

*D*on't judge a book by it's cover is an old adage that clearly applies to jícama. Its rough exterior may be off-putting but underneath that layer lies a sweet, crunchy vegetable with a flavor that hints at cucumber and potato. Look for jícama in larger produce sections or in markets that specialize in Mexican food.

MAKES 4 SERVINGS

¾	pound tuna fillet	12	baby artichokes, trimmed, cooked, and quartered, or 12 artichoke hearts packed in brine, drained and quartered
½	teaspoon salt, or to taste		
¼	teaspoon freshly ground black pepper, or to taste		
6	tablespoons extra-virgin olive oil	1	jícama, peeled and julienned
2	tablespoons balsamic vinegar	1	red, yellow, or green pepper, roasted, peeled, and cut into strips (page 191)
2	teaspoons freshly squeezed lime juice		
1	tablespoon chopped fresh cilantro	8	sun-dried tomatoes, reconstituted (page 191) and julienned

1. Prepare a charcoal fire or preheat a gas grill on high.
2. Pat the tuna dry, season it lightly with salt and pepper, and brush with a little of the olive oil. When the charcoal is white-hot or the gas grill fully preheated, grill the tuna for 1 to 2 minutes per side, or until just cooked through; remove it from the grill and cut it into an even dice of about 1 to 2 inches.
3. Combine the remaining olive oil, vinegar, lime juice, cilantro, and salt and pepper to taste in a bowl.
4. Add the tuna, artichokes, jícama, roasted pepper, and sun-dried tomatoes. Toss to coat evenly. Let the salad marinate, covered, in the refrigerator for 1 to 2 hours.
5. Serve the salad on chilled plates.

Nutrition information, per serving: 535 calories, 31 grams protein, 25 grams fat, 55 grams carbohydrates, 580 milligrams sodium, 30 milligrams cholesterol.

Serving Suggestions: To make this salad into a lunch or summer supper main course, add some grilled Basic Flatbread (page 152), and serve it on a bed of greens. Add additional vegetables (raw, grilled, or lightly steamed) such as green beans, broccoli, or bell peppers. Garnish with olives.

Spinach Salad with Warm Poppy Seed Dressing

This salad, with its Pennsylvania Dutch-inspired sweet and sour dressing, is assembled very quickly. Use the largest skillet you have to hold the spinach easily, or a wok. If necessary, cook it in two batches.

MAKES 6 SERVINGS

4	tablespoons sherry vinegar		4	tablespoons olive or walnut oil
1	cup sliced white mushrooms		1	tablespoon honey
½	teaspoon salt		1	tablespoon poppyseeds
	Freshly ground black pepper to taste		1	orange, peeled and thinly sliced
2	(10-ounce) bags spinach, or 1 ½ pounds loose leaf spinach			

1. Whisk together 2 tablespoons of the sherry vinegar and salt and pepper to taste, add the mushrooms, and set aside to marinate.

2. Rinse the spinach well to remove all sand, remove stems, and dry well.

3. Heat the oil, remaining vinegar, honey, poppy seeds, and salt and pepper in a large skillet over medium heat until very warm, but not boiling.

4. Add the spinach all at once and toss just until the leaves wilt very slightly.

5. Transfer the spinach mixture to a serving bowl or individual plates, top with the mushrooms and arrange the sliced orange around the salad.

NUTRITION INFORMATION, PER SERVING: 135 calories, 3 grams protein, 10 grams fat, 10 grams carbohydrates, 254 milligrams sodium, 0 milligrams cholesterol.

VARIATIONS: Add diced cooked bacon, croutons, or slivered carrots.

SERVING SUGGESTIONS: This is a fine choice to accompany grilled or sautéed fish or chicken, and could be used as a bed beneath grilled fish or chicken or as a side dish.

Herb-Cured Salmon with Clementines and Horseradish Mustard

*T*his easy preparation yields spectacular results, but it requires a three-day curing period, so plan ahead.

Clementines belong to the zipper skin family of citrus, a variety of mandarin orange similar to the tangerine, but seedless. They are available from November through April, with a high point that coincides with the winter holidays.

MAKES 10–12 SERVINGS

1 pound salmon fillet, skin left on	¼ cup chopped fennel leaves (optional)
2 tablespoons kosher or sea salt	1 tablespoon brandy
¼ cup light brown sugar	6 cups cleaned assorted greens
1 tablespoon freshly ground black pepper	¾ cup Balsamic Vinaigrette (page 14)
2 tablespoons dried or fresh thyme leaves	3 clementines, peeled and separated into segments
½ cup chopped fresh dill	6 tablespoons Horseradish Mustard (page 132)

1. Pat the salmon dry with paper towels. Check for pin bones by running your finger down the length of the fillet and remove them with needle-nosed pliers or sturdy tweezers, or ask the butcher to remove them for you.

2. Mix together the salt, brown sugar, and black pepper. Sprinkle the mixture on both sides of the salmon, rubbing it in well. Arrange the salmon, skin side down on a large piece of plastic wrap. Sprinkle the herbs and brandy over the flesh, then wrap it tightly in the plastic wrap.

3. Place the wrapped salmon in a clean baking dish, top with a second baking dish, and weight it down with a couple of cans or bricks. Place the salmon in the refrigerator to cure for three days.

4. Unwrap the salmon, scrape away the herbs and spices, and blot it dry. Slice the salmon very thinly, using a sharp slicing knife and cutting on a sharp diagonal. Arrange the slices on individual plates or on one side of a serving platter.

5. Lightly toss the greens with the vinaigrette in a bowl. Mound the greens next to the salmon.

6. Garnish with the clementine segments and serve with Horseradish Mustard.

NUTRITION INFORMATION, PER SERVING: 215 calories, 25 grams protein, 9 grams fat, 9 grams carbohydrates, 1,900 milligrams sodium, 65 milligrams cholesterol.

VARIATIONS: When clementines are not available, use tangerines or any good eating orange. Blood oranges, with their rich ruby red color, add an especially dramatic touch.

SERVING SUGGESTIONS: This item is excellent as part of an hors d'oeuvre buffet or as a first course in a formal dinner party. Serve it with toasted slices of French bread, warm brioche, or crisp Basic Flatbread (page 152).

WILD MUSHROOM-POTATO CAKES

*T*he wild mushrooms available in your area may vary according to the season. Morels, chanterelles, oyster mushrooms, and shiitakes all have subtly unique flavors. Look for fresh, moist but not damp mushrooms with a woodsy aroma.

MAKES 4 SERVINGS

3	Idaho potatoes, peeled and diced		1	egg, slightly beaten
2	tablespoons butter		½	teaspoon salt, or to taste
1	tablespoon minced shallots		¼	teaspoon freshly ground black pepper,
½	pound shiitake mushrooms, stems			or to taste
	removed and thinly sliced		½	cup vegetable oil

1. Place the potatoes in a saucepan and add enough cool water to cover. Bring to a simmer over high heat and cook the potatoes until fork tender, about 20 minutes. Drain the potatoes in a colander, return them to the pan, and steam dry over low heat, shaking the pan occasionally, for 2 to 3 minutes. Transfer the potatoes to a mixing bowl.

2. Heat the butter in a skillet over medium heat. Add the shallots and mushrooms, and cook over high heat until the mushrooms are tender and any moisture they release has cooked away, 6 to 8 minutes.

3. Add the mushrooms and shallots to the potatoes. Add the egg, salt, and pepper, and stir to combine. When the mixture is cool enough to handle, shape it into 4 large or 8 small cakes.

4. Heat about ¼ inch of the vegetable oil in a skillet over high heat. Add the potato cakes and cook for about 2 to 3 minutes on the first side, or until golden brown. Turn the cakes; reduce heat to medium and cook 2 to 3 minutes or until golden brown.

5. Drain the cakes briefly on paper towels and serve while still very hot.

NUTRITION INFORMATION, PER SERVING (1 LARGE OR 2 SMALL CAKES): 205 calories, 5 grams protein, 16 grams fat, 500 milligrams sodium, 36 milligrams cholesterol.

An American Bounty

VARIATION: Chopped fresh seasonal herbs such as thyme or basil may be added in step 3 for extra flavor.

SERVING SUGGESTIONS: Top these flavorful savory pancakes with the traditional applesauce and sour cream or with a fresh or dried cherry compote. Serve them as a side dish for roasted pork or beef or as an elegant first course. At brunch, they make an excellent entrée topped with smoked salmon.

STEAMED MAINE MUSSELS WITH SPICY RED CURRY

Mussels are among the farm-raised types of shellfish that can be found in most markets and fish stores throughout the country. Good mussels should be sweet, briny-tasting, plump, and delicately flavored. This rich, vibrantly colored sauce looks beautiful with coral-colored mussels in their black shells.

MAKES 4 SERVINGS

60 Maine mussels	½ cup Red Curry Paste (page 131)
1 tablespoon peanut oil	2 cups canned coconut milk
3 garlic cloves, minced	¼ cup finely chopped fresh cilantro leaves
1 tablespoon minced gingerroot	
2 plum tomatoes, peeled, seeded, and diced (page 191)	½ bunch scallions, cut on the bias

1. Scrub the mussels under cold water and remove their beards.

2. Heat the peanut oil in a saucepan. Add the garlic, ginger, and tomatoes, and cook over low heat, stirring frequently, for 5 minutes.

3. Add the curry paste and coconut milk. Stir to blend evenly and bring to a simmer over medium heat.

4. Add the mussels, cover the pan, and cook over medium heat for about 6 minutes, or until the mussels have steamed open. Discard any mussels that do not open.

5. Use a slotted spoon to transfer the mussels to heated soup plates or a deep platter. Add the chopped cilantro and scallions to the broth in the pan, and ladle the broth over the mussels. Serve at once.

NUTRITION INFORMATION, PER SERVING: 460 calories, 17 grams protein, 38 grams fat, 18 grams carbohydrates, 450 milligrams sodium, 30 milligrams cholesterol.

PREPARATION NOTES: Mussels do not last long under refrigeration; cook them within a day or two. Check them carefully as you scrub them. Discard any open ones that do not close when you gently rap them on a counter.

Be sure to purchase canned coconut milk. Coconut cream, used to make drinks such as piña coladas, is too sweet.

LOWER-FAT VERSION: Reduced-fat coconut milk is available and will make no difference in the flavor of this dish but will reduce the fat by half.

SERVING SUGGESTIONS: This makes an excellent first course for a dinner built around Asian flavors, but it would also make a fine entrée. To round it out, serve the mussels with plenty of steamed rice or cooked noodles and a few refreshing salads.

Potato Gnocchi with Pumpkin, Spinach, and Shiitake Mushrooms

Gnocchi is the Italian name for bite-sized dumplings. This autumn variation of a traditional Italian dish relies on the earthy flavors of wild mushrooms and pumpkin cooked in a *beurre noisette.*

MAKES 4 SERVINGS

2	Idaho potatoes, peeled and diced
1	egg yolk, lightly beaten
1	tablespoon extra-virgin olive oil
½	teaspoon salt, or to taste
½ to ⅔	cup all-purpose flour
2	cups pumpkin cubes (1-inch)
2	tablespoons butter
6 to 8	shiitake mushrooms, stems removed, cleaned, and sliced (about 1 cup)
12	ounces spinach leaves, thoroughly rinsed, drained, and stems removed
2	tablespoons grated dry Monterey Jack cheese

1. Place the potatoes in a saucepan and add enough cold water to cover. Bring to a simmer over medium heat and cook until fork tender, about 20 minutes. Drain the potatoes, return them to the pan, and steam dry, shaking the pan occasionally, for 2 to 3 minutes.

2. Push the potatoes through a sieve or food mill. Immediately stir the yolk, oil, salt, and ½ cup of flour into the potatoes. Beat with a wooden spoon until the flour is blended into the potatoes.

3. Turn the dough onto a lightly floured work surface and knead, gradually adding just enough of the remaining flour to create a smooth pliable dough; it should feel just slightly sticky. Allow the mixture to cool.

4. Divide the dough into two pieces and roll them into logs about 1 inch in diameter. Cut the logs into ½-inch pieces. Roll the pieces gently along the inner curves of a fork to complete shaping the gnocchi.

5. Bring a pot of lightly salted water to a rolling boil over high heat.

6. Meanwhile, bring 1 inch of water to a boil in a saucepan with a steamer insert. Place the pumpkin in the steamer, cover, and steam until barely tender, 25 to 30 minutes. Uncover and remove from heat.

7. Melt the butter in a skillet over medium-high heat, and continue to cook it until there is a distinctly nutty aroma and the butter has just begun to turn brown; do not let the butter burn. Add the mushrooms and sauté for 2 to 3 minutes, just until soft.

8. Add the pumpkin and spinach to the skillet and cook over high heat, stirring from time to time, for 2 minutes.

9. Lower the heat under the water to reduce it to a simmer. Add the gnocchi to the pot. As the gnocchi rise to the surface of the water, remove them with a slotted spoon.

10. Add the drained gnocchi to the pumpkin-mushroom mixture and toss until they are evenly combined.

11. Serve at once on a heated platter or individual plates and top with the grated cheese.

NUTRITION INFORMATION, PER SERVING (¾ CUP): 300 calories, 10 grams protein, 12 grams fat, 42 grams carbohydrates, 550 milligrams sodium, 22 milligrams cholesterol.

VARIATIONS: Other wild mushrooms, such as cremini or portobello, can be used in place of the shiitake. Winter squash may be substituted for the pumpkin.

SERVING SUGGESTIONS: This makes a wonderful prelude to a main course of Roasted Game Hens (page 84). Or, double the portion size, and serve this as an entrée preceded by a platter of steamed asparagus or green beans.

TOMATO SAMPLER WITH PAN-FRIED CALAMARI

Calamari, or squid, belongs to a group of fish known as cephalopods, or "head-footed," since it appears that their feet, or tentacles, grow directly from their heads. It is delicious, mild-flavored, and firm-textured. Ask your fishmonger to remove the ink sac, as well as the "quill" that are found inside the calamari body.

MAKES 4 SERVINGS

¾ pound fresh calamari

½ cup all-purpose flour, or as needed for dredging

2 teaspoons Old Bay seafood seasoning

½ teaspoon salt, or to taste

¼ teaspoon freshly ground black pepper, or to taste

½ cup milk

½ cup vegetable oil, or as needed for pan-frying

1 bunch arugula, stems removed, rinsed, and thoroughly dried

½ head frisée, trimmed, rinsed, torn into pieces, and thoroughly dried

½ cup Balsamic Vinaigrette (page 14)

1 yellow beefsteak tomato, thickly sliced

1 red beefsteak tomato, thickly sliced

¼ pint red cherry tomatoes, halved

¼ pint yellow cherry tomatoes, halved

1. To prepare the calamari, cut the body into rings approximately ⅛ inch thick. Rinse the rings and tentacles well in cold water, then blot dry on paper towels.

2. Combine the flour, Old Bay seasoning, salt, and pepper in a large plate or pan. Pour the milk into a shallow bowl.

3. Add the oil to a skillet (there should be about ¼ inch covering the bottom) and preheat over medium-high heat.

4. Dip the squid rings and tentacles first into the milk and then into the seasoned flour, turning to coat evenly. Immediately lower the rings into the hot oil using a slotted spoon. Cook, turning occasionally, until the squid is golden brown on all sides, 6 to 8 minutes.

5. Remove the calamari from the oil and drain briefly on paper towels.

6. Toss the arugula and frisée with ¼ cup of the vinaigrette and mound the dressed greens on a serving platter or on individual plates. Add the tomatoes and the remaining vinaigrette in the bowl and very gently toss to coat.

7. Top the greens with the tomatoes and calamari. Serve at once.

NUTRITION INFORMATION. PER SERVING: 355 calories, 18 grams protein, 24 grams fat, 20 grams carbohydrates, 970 milligrams sodium, 225 milligrams cholesterol.

VARIATIONS: If arugula and frisée are not available, use romaine, red or green leaf lettuce, escarole, or chicory.

In place of Balsamic Vinaigrette, Sherry Wine Vinaigrette or Mustard and Roasted Garlic Vinaigrette can be used (pages 14–15).

SERVING SUGGESTIONS: This dish is well-suited to a starring role for lunch or dinner, and requires only some hearty, whole-grain rolls or bread to round out the meal.

Dip rings of sliced red or Vidalia onions into the milk, then into the seasoned flour, and fry them in the oil. Scatter the onion rings over the squid.

Overleaf:
Tomato Sampler
with Pan-Fried
Calamari

SOFT-SHELL CRABS WITH PECANS, DILL, AND GRAPEFRUIT

*T*he trick here is to have both the pan and the oil very hot and to be sure not to crowd the crabs in the pan—sauté only one or two at a time, if necessary. The results will be worth the little extra effort.

MAKES 4 SERVINGS

4	soft-shell crabs, cleaned		2	tablespoons vegetable oil or clarified butter (or more)
½	cup all-purpose flour, or as needed to dredge crabs		2	tablespoons unsalted butter
1	teaspoon Old Bay seafood seasoning, or to taste		12	grapefruit sections, preferably pink; juices reserved
¼	teaspoon kosher salt, or to taste		3	ounces toasted pecans (page 192)
¼	teaspoon freshly ground black pepper, or to taste		2	tablespoons chopped fresh dill

1. Pat the crabs dry with paper towels. Combine the flour with the Old Bay seasoning, salt, and pepper; dredge the crabs lightly in the flour and shake off any excess.

2. Heat the oil or clarified butter in a skillet over high heat. Add the crabs, backs down first, to the oil. Do not add more than can fit without touching.

3. Sauté the crabs for 2 minutes, or until they are deep golden brown. Turn and sauté for another 2 minutes; transfer to a warm baking dish or serving platter.

4. Pour any excess oil from the skillet. Return the skillet to medium-high heat. Add the butter and swirl it in the pan constantly until it begins to brown, about 1 minute.

5. Add the grapefruit sections and juice, the pecans, and the dill. Cook for 3 minutes more, and remove from the heat.

6. Place the crabs on a heated platter or individual plates, and pour the sauce over and around them. Serve at once.

NUTRITION INFORMATION, PER CRAB: 230 calories, 5 grams protein, 22 grams fat, 8 grams carbohydrates, 340 milligrams sodium, 60 milligrams cholesterol.

PREPARATION NOTES: Soft-shell crabs do need some advance cleaning. Turn the crab over and pull away the apron covering the stomach. Cut away the eyes and squeeze gently to expel the green bubble. If you are unsure about how to do this, ask the fishmonger to clean the crabs for you.

Soft-shell crabs are a highly perishable food, so cook them within a day of purchase.

SERVING SUGGESTIONS: Serve 1 crab as an appetizer, paired with a Riesling or a Gewürztraminer.

For an entrée, serve 2 crabs per person on a bed of rice pilaf.

Pasta with Sautéed Country Ham, Apples, and Hazelnuts

*H*azelnuts, or filberts as they also are known, have a rich buttery flavor that marries beautifully with country ham. You often can find shelled hazelnuts in health-food stores. Prolonged storage at room temperature shortens the shelf life of these nuts, so buy them in small quantities at shops that have brisk sales and taste them for freshness before using.

MAKES 4 SERVINGS

1 teaspoon extra-virgin olive oil	¼ teaspoon freshly ground black pepper
4 ounces country-style ham, julienned	1 teaspoon salt, or to taste
1 Granny Smith apple, thinly sliced	½ pound fresh linguini or fettuccine
½ cup heavy cream	¼ cup toasted hazelnuts (page 192)

1. Bring a pot of water to a boil over high heat.

2. Heat the olive oil in a skillet over medium heat. Add the ham and cook, stirring frequently, for 2 to 3 minutes. Add the apple and cream, and simmer gently over low heat, stirring from time to time, until the cream thickens slightly, 5 to 6 minutes. Add pepper and keep the mixture warm.

3. Add the salt to the water, drop in the pasta, and stir once or twice with a fork to separate the strands.

4. When the pasta is just tender to the bite, drain it well in a colander. Add the pasta to the skillet, and toss it gently over low heat until it is evenly coated with the sauce. Serve at once in heated bowls or plates. Garnish with the hazelnuts.

NUTRITION INFORMATION, PER SERVING (¾ CUP): 480 calories, 15 grams protein, 26 grams fat, 49 grams carbohydrates, 225 milligrams sodium, 60 milligrams cholesterol.

PREPARATION NOTES: If you are making your own pasta, replace ¼ to ⅓ cup of the flour with finely ground toasted hazelnuts.

Soups

*T*his stew is a variation of the popular oyster stew that has been served at New York's Grand Central Terminal Oyster Bar since 1912.

MAKES 6 TO 8 SERVINGS

8	ounces shucked oysters with their juices	1	bay leaf
2	bacon slices, minced	½	cup heavy cream, warmed
1	onion, minced	½	teaspoon salt, or to taste
2	tablespoons flour	¼	teaspoon freshly ground black pepper, or to taste
3	cups milk		Oyster crackers

1. Drain the oysters in a colander set over a bowl. Reserve the juice.

2. Sauté the bacon in a large pot over medium heat until it is crisp and the fat is rendered. Remove the bacon with a slotted spoon and reserve.

3. Sauté the onions in bacon fat until tender and translucent, but not brown, about 5 minutes.

4. Add flour, and cook over low heat for 3 to 4 minutes, stirring constantly with a wooden spoon.

5. Add the milk and reserved oyster juice gradually, whisking constantly to prevent any lumps from forming.

6. Add the bay leaf and simmer for 20 minutes, skimming as necessary.

7. Add the oysters and simmer another 5 minutes, or just until the oysters are barely cooked. Take care not to overcook the oysters.

8. Add the warm cream and adjust seasoning with salt and pepper.

9. Ladle the soup into heated bowls and garnish with reserved bacon and oyster crackers.

NUTRITION INFORMATION, PER SERVING (6 OUNCES): 190 calories, 8 grams protein, 12 grams fat, 13 grams carbohydrates, 110 milligrams sodium, 55 milligrams cholesterol.

Preceding Page:
Oyster Stew

TOMATO AND SWEET PEPPER SOUP

When peppers and tomatoes begin to ripen in late summer into fall, this soup is a good way to showcase their wonderful flavors.

MAKES 6 TO 8 SERVINGS

2 tablespoons olive oil

1 onion, finely diced

2 garlic cloves, minced

2 sweet red bell peppers, seeds and ribs removed, and julienned

2 celery stalks, thinly sliced

3 tomatoes, peeled, seeded, and chopped (page 191)

6 cups chicken broth (page 193)

¼ cup heavy cream

1 tablespoon poppy seeds

½ teaspoon salt, or to taste

¼ teaspoon freshly ground black pepper, or to taste

1. Heat the oil in a soup pot over medium heat.

2. Add the onions and garlic, and stir to coat evenly with the oil. Cover the pot and let the onions cook over low heat for 6 to 8 minutes or until they are soft and translucent, but not browned.

3. Add the peppers, celery, and tomatoes to the pot, replace the cover, and continue to cook until the vegetables are limp, 6 to 8 minutes.

4. Add the broth, bring to a full boil, then reduce the heat to low. Simmer the soup for 20 minutes or until the vegetables are tender.

5. While the soup is simmering, whip the cream to soft peaks and fold in the poppy seeds.

6. Taste the soup and adjust the seasoning with salt and pepper.

7. Serve the soup topped with the poppy seed whipped cream.

NUTRITION INFORMATION, PER SERVING (6 OUNCES): 210 calories, 5 grams protein, 18 grams fat, 9 grams carbohydrates, 115 milligrams sodium, 35 milligrams cholesterol.

VARIATIONS: Substitute combinations of red, green, and yellow peppers and tomatoes. Omit the cream and add to each serving a curl or two of Parmesan cheese or a Cheddar Rusk (page 52).

CHESTNUT SOUP WITH FRESH GINGER

*H*istorically, chestnuts were an important part of the diet of American Indians as an excellent source of protein and carbohydrates. Today, chestnuts are favored not only for their wonderful flavor, but also for their nearly total lack of fat, a rarity in nuts. This would make a wonderful first course for a winter or fall dinner party, or a Thanksgiving feast.

MAKES 4 TO 6 SERVINGS

10	ounces chestnuts (in shell)
1	tablespoon unsalted butter
½	onion, diced
1	celery stalk, diced
1	carrot, diced
1	leek, white and light green portions only, chopped
4	cups chicken broth (page 193)

2	tablespoons peeled and grated ginger-root
2	tablespoons freshly squeezed orange juice
¾	cup heavy cream
½	teaspoon salt, or to taste
¼	teaspoon freshly ground black pepper, or to taste

1. Preheat the oven to 400 degrees F or bring a large pot of water to a rolling boil.

2. Score an "X" on the flat side of each chestnut with the tip of a sharp paring knife. Place them on a baking sheet and roast them in the oven or boil them until the outer skin begins to curl away, 10 to 12 minutes. Peel away both the outer and inner layers of skin from the chestnuts.

3. Chop the chestnuts coarsely with a chef's knife and reserve.

4. Heat the butter in a soup pot over medium-high heat. Add the onion, celery, carrot, and leek, and sauté, stirring frequently, until the onion is a light, golden brown, 8 to 10 minutes.

5. Add the broth, chopped chestnuts, and ginger. Bring the soup to a full boil, then immediately reduce the heat to low and simmer, uncovered, stirring from time to time, until all the ingredients are very tender, 35 to 40 minutes. Remove from the heat and cool slightly.

6. Purée the soup using a hand-held immersion blender or in a food processor or blender.

7. Return the soup to medium heat, add the orange juice, and simmer for 2 minutes.

8. Warm the cream over low heat or in a microwave oven, then add it to the soup. Adjust the seasoning with salt, pepper, and orange juice if necessary. Serve at once in a heated tureen or individual bowls.

NUTRITION INFORMATION, PER SERVING (6 OUNCES): 245 calories, 4 grams protein, 15 grams fat, 25 grams carbohydrates, 285 milligrams sodium, 50 milligrams cholesterol.

PREPARATION NOTES: It is easiest to peel chestnuts while they are still warm. If necessary, rewarm the nuts by dropping them back into simmering water or returning them to a warm oven.

The soup may be completed through step 7, then refrigerated for up to 4 days, or frozen for up to 4 weeks. Bring the soup back to a full boil and, if necessary, adjust the thickness by adding some hot broth or water. Then, continue with the final step.

VARIATION: For an elegant garnish, whip a little sour cream or crème fraîche with some grated fresh gingerroot to taste, and place a dollop on each serving.

Manhattan Clam Chowder

*T*his is the classic mid-Atlantic clam chowder, not to be confused with New England's version. So controversial was the inclusion of tomatoes to New Englanders that a piece of legislation attempting to ban tomatoes from any true chowder was once introduced in Maine.

MAKES 6 TO 8 SERVINGS

- 2 dozen cherrystone clams, shucked, juices reserved
- 2 bacon slices, minced
- 1 onion, diced
- 1 carrot, chopped
- 1 celery stalk, chopped
- ¼ cup sliced leeks
- 1 bell pepper, red or green, seeded and diced
- 2 garlic cloves, minced
- 2 cups clam broth
- 3 plum tomatoes, peeled, seeded, and chopped (page 191)
- 1 cup tomato juice
- 2 potatoes, peeled and diced
- 1 sprig fresh thyme, or ½ teaspoon dried leaves
- 1 sprig fresh marjoram, or ½ teaspoon dried leaves
- 1 bay leaf
- 7 to 8 cracked black peppercorns
- ½ teaspoon salt, or to taste

1. Chop the clams into large pieces. Cook the bacon in a soup pot over medium heat until it is crisp, about 5 minutes.

2. Add the onion, carrot, celery, leeks, pepper, and garlic; stir to coat evenly with the bacon fat. Cover the pot and cook over low heat until the onion is translucent, 6 to 8 minutes. Add the clam broth, reserved juices, tomatoes, and tomato juice, and bring to a simmer.

3. Add the potatoes, thyme, marjoram, bay leaf, and peppercorns. Simmer over low heat for 15 to 20 minutes, or until the potatoes are tender.

4. Add the clams and simmer for 5 minutes more or until the clams are tender and cooked just until their edges have curled slightly; do not overcook, or the clams will toughen.

5. Adjust the seasonings and serve in a heated tureen or individual bowls.

NUTRITION INFORMATION, PER SERVING (6 OUNCES): 195 calories, 18 grams protein, 6 grams fat, 18 grams carbohydrates, 230 milligrams sodium, 25 milligrams cholesterol.

CHILLED POTATO-BASIL SOUP

*T*his soup is based on the classic vichysoisse that was first prepared by Louis Diat and served at the Ritz-Carlton Hotel in New York. That soup was itself an Americanized version of a favorite soup made by Chef Diat's mother.

MAKES 4 TO 6 SERVINGS

1	bacon slice, chopped
1	yellow onion, chopped
2	Idaho potatoes, peeled and sliced
4	cups chicken broth (page 193)
1	bay leaf
½	cup half-and-half (optional)
½	teaspoon salt, or to taste

¼	teaspoon freshly ground black pepper, or to taste
	Tabasco or similar hot pepper sauce to taste
1	plum tomato, finely diced
2	tablespoons shredded fresh basil

1. Cook the bacon in a soup pot over medium heat until the fat is rendered and the bacon is crisp, about 5 minutes.

2. Add the onions and sauté, stirring frequently, until they are tender and translucent, 6 to 8 minutes.

3. Add the potatoes, broth, and bay leaf, and simmer until the potatoes are tender enough to pierce easily with a fork.

4. Remove and discard the bay leaf.

5. Let the soup cool slightly and then purée it in a blender or food processor until smooth. Transfer the soup to a bowl, cool to room temperature, and refrigerate overnight.

6. If necessary, the consistency of the soup may be adjusted by adding additional broth or water. Add half-and-half to the chilled soup if desired, then taste for the seasoning. Add salt, pepper, and Tabasco to taste. Top with diced tomato and basil.

NUTRITION INFORMATION, PER SERVING (6 OUNCES): 100 calories, 5 grams protein, 4 grams fat, 13 grams carbohydrates, 245 milligrams sodium, 15 milligrams cholesterol.

VARIATIONS: This soup also can be served hot. Oregano, tarragon, or chives can be substituted for the basil.

NEW CORN CHOWDER

Simmering the corn cobs in broth gives the soup a deep corn flavor.

MAKES 8 SERVINGS

6	ears corn on the cob, husked	1	red pepper, roasted, peeled, seeded,
4	cups chicken broth (page 193)		and diced (page 191)
2	tablespoons butter	3	scallions, thinly sliced on the bias
1	onion, diced		Tabasco or similar hot pepper sauce
2	tablespoons all-purpose flour		Cider vinegar
2	Idaho potatoes, peeled and diced		Salt to taste
2	ounces cured ham, diced		Freshly ground black pepper to taste

1. Cut the kernels from the cob and set them aside. Place the cobs in a soup pot and cover with the broth. Bring to a simmer over medium heat and simmer gently for about 30 minutes.

2. Discard the corn cobs and strain the broth.

3. Return the soup pot to medium heat and heat the butter. Add the onion and sauté, stirring frequently, until limp. Add the flour and continue to cook, stirring, for another 5 minutes.

4. Add the broth to the onion mixture, whisking to remove any lumps; bring to a simmer.

5. Add the potatoes and corn kernels. Simmer for 20 minutes, until the potatoes are tender.

6. Add the diced ham and pepper, and continue to simmer for 5 minutes more.

7. Add the scallions and season to taste with Tabasco, vinegar, salt, and pepper.

NUTRITION INFORMATION, PER SERVING (6 OUNCES): 175 calories, 8 grams protein, 5 grams fat, 27 grams carbohydrates, 490 milligrams sodium, 10 milligrams cholesterol.

PREPARATION NOTES: This soup can be prepared in advance through step 6, then refrigerated or frozen. Return the soup to a simmer before adding the scallions and seasonings.

SERVING SUGGESTIONS: Make a smooth purée of avocado and squirt it over the soup in a random pattern, or add chunks of avocado at the last moment. Cut corn tortillas into wedges, toast them in a hot oven until crisp, and float them on the soup.

BUTTERNUT AND
ACORN SQUASH SOUP

*T*his soup has a rich creamy texture that belies its actual calorie count. Feel free to use only one type of squash or to replace some or all of the squash with pumpkin.

MAKES 4 TO 6 SERVINGS

1	tablespoon unsalted butter	2	cups cubed butternut squash
1	onion, diced	1	cup cubed acorn squash
1	carrot, diced	½	potato, peeled and sliced
1	celery stalk, trimmed and diced	½	teaspoon salt, or to taste
1	clove garlic, peeled and minced	¼	teaspoon freshly ground black pepper,
1	teaspoon ground ginger		or to taste
3 to 4	cups chicken broth (page 193)	1	teaspoon julienned orange zest

1. Heat the butter in a soup pot over medium heat.

2. Add the onion, carrot, celery, and garlic, and sauté, stirring frequently, until the onion is tender and translucent, 5 to 6 minutes.

3. Add the ginger and sauté for another minute.

4. Add the broth, squashes, and potato. Bring the broth to a full boil over medium heat, then reduce the heat to low and simmer until the squashes are tender enough to pierce easily with a fork, about 20 minutes.

5. Remove the soup from the heat and allow it to cool briefly. Purée the soup with a hand-held immersion blender, or in a food processor or blender, or by pushing it through a sieve or food mill.

6. Return the soup to the pot and bring to a simmer. Adjust the consistency if necessary by adding additional broth or water. Taste the soup and add salt, pepper, and orange zest.

7. Serve the soup in a heated tureen or individual bowls.

NUTRITION INFORMATION, PER SERVING (6 OUNCES): 180 calories, 4 grams protein, 10 grams fat, 18 grams carbohydrates, 285 milligrams sodium, 40 milligrams cholesterol.

PREPARATION NOTES: To give this soup a more pronounced orange taste, add a tablespoon of frozen orange juice concentrate with the final flavor adjustment. A few drops of lemon or lime juice would also brighten the flavor.

AHEAD OF TIME: To make this soup in advance, complete the recipe through step 5. Cool the soup to room temperature, transfer to a bowl or other storage container, cover, and refrigerate or freeze. The soup can be held in the refrigerator for up to 3 days, or frozen for up to a month. Before serving, return the soup to a full boil, then make the final adjustments to consistency and flavoring.

SERVING SUGGESTIONS: Whip a little heavy cream to soft peaks, fold in an equal amount of sour cream, and add freshly grated gingerroot to taste. Place a dollop on each portion.

This soup can be served chilled. After cooling, refrigerate for several hours or overnight. Garnish each portion with a thin slice of orange.

SEAFOOD GUMBO

*G*umbos are among the most famous dishes of southern Louisiana. These spicy soup/stews typically include okra and tomatoes and are thickened with a roux. Some versions, such as the one here, incorporate spicy Andouille sausage and a variety of shellfish. Others are built from a collection of game meats. Still others have no meat at all, and are made by simmering a combination of "pot greens," such as dandelion, collard, mustard, and turnip greens, in a savory broth.

MAKES 10 SERVINGS

⅓ cup clarified butter or vegetable oil	8 cups fish broth (page 193) or chicken broth (page 193)
⅔ cup flour	1½ cups tomato sauce (homemade or canned)
1 onion, diced	
1 stalk celery, diced	1 cup diced Andouille sausage
1 green pepper, seeded and diced	2 cups sliced fresh okra
3 cloves garlic, minced	2 plum tomatoes, peeled, seeded, and diced (page 191)
Several dashes of Tabasco or similar hot pepper sauce	16–20 oysters, shucked, liquor reserved
½ teaspoon ground white pepper	¾ pound cleaned crabmeat
¼ teaspoon garlic powder	¾ pound peeled, deveined, medium shrimp
¼ teaspoon freshly ground black pepper	
¼ teaspoon hot paprika	Salt to taste
¼ teaspoon dried thyme leaves	Cayenne pepper to taste
½ teaspoon dried oregano leaves	

1. Heat the butter or oil in a soup pot over medium heat. Stir in the flour and cook, stirring constantly, until the roux is a very dark brown, but not burned, about 15 minutes.

2. Add the onion, celery, and green pepper, and cook over high heat for about 5 minutes, stirring constantly. Add the garlic, hot pepper sauce, and dried spices. Continue to cook, stirring constantly, for another 2 minutes.

3. Add the broth and tomato sauce gradually, whisking constantly to work out any lumps. When they are completely incorporated, bring the soup to a boil, reduce the heat, and simmer for 45 minutes.

4. Meanwhile, bring about ½ inch of water to a boil in a skillet. Add the sausage and cook over low heat, covered, for 5 to 6 minutes. Remove the sausage and drain well on paper towels.

5. Add the sausage, okra, and tomatoes to the soup and simmer another 10 minutes.

6. Add the shellfish and the reserved liquor and simmer just until it is barely cooked through, 4 to 5 minutes.

7. Adjust the seasoning to taste with salt, cayenne pepper, and additional hot pepper sauce.

NUTRITION INFORMATION, PER SERVING (6 OUNCES): 300 calories, 24 grams protein, 16 grams fat, 17 grams carbohydrates, 140 milligrams sodium, 110 milligrams cholesterol.

PREPARATION NOTES: To be sure that you don't overcook the shellfish, try this method: Add the oysters and their liquor, the crabmeat, and shrimp to the soup, and bring it just back to a low boil. Cover the pot and remove it from the heat; set aside for 10 minutes. The shellfish should be fully cooked but still tender.

SERVING SUGGESTION: Plain boiled or steamed white rice is traditional.

Zucchini Soup with Cheddar Rusks

*A*dding a rusk to each bowl of soup hearkens back to some of the original "soupes," when bread played a more integral role. Like French onion soup, this dish has a unique texture and flavor that can become addictive.

Makes 6 to 8 servings

2	bacon strips, minced		2	tablespoons tarragon or cider vinegar
1	onion, diced		6 to 8	slices of French or Italian bread
2	garlic cloves, minced		½	cup grated Cheddar cheese
2	medium zucchini, diced (3 to 4 cups)		1	tablespoon minced fresh basil
3	cups chicken broth (page 193)		½	teaspoon salt, or to taste
2	plum tomatoes, peeled, seeded, and chopped (page 191)		¼	teaspoon freshly ground black pepper, or to taste
¼	cup tomato purée			

1. Cook the bacon in a soup pot over medium heat until the fat is rendered and the bacon bits are crisp, about 5 minutes.

2. Add the onions and garlic, and sauté, stirring frequently, until the onions are a light golden brown, 8 to 10 minutes.

3. Add the zucchini, cover the pot, and cook for 5 minutes, or until the zucchini start to become translucent.

4. Add the broth, tomatoes, tomato purée, and vinegar, and bring the soup to a boil over high heat. Reduce the heat to low and simmer for 15 to 20 minutes, or until all the vegetables are very tender and the soup has developed a good flavor.

5. While the soup is simmering, prepare the rusks: Toast the bread slices on a baking sheet under a preheated broiler, turning once, until golden brown on both sides. Scatter the cheese evenly over the second side of the toasted bread and continue to broil just until the cheese bubbles and begins to brown.

6. Add the basil to the soup and adjust the seasoning with salt and pepper.

7. Serve the soup in a heated tureen or individual bowls. Top each serving with a Cheddar rusk.

NUTRITION INFORMATION, PER SERVING (6 OUNCES): 70 calories, 5 grams protein, 2 grams fat, 9 grams carbohydrates, 85 milligrams sodium, 5 milligrams cholesterol.

PREPARATION NOTES: When zucchini become large, their seeds can become a little bitter. If you are using a giant-sized squash, cut it in half lengthwise, scoop out and discard the seeds with a tablespoon, then dice the flesh. Smaller zucchini can be used seeds and all.

AHEAD OF TIME: The rusks can be made well in advance and warmed slightly just before serving.

VARIATION: For a vegetarian soup, omit the bacon and add a tablespoon or two of olive oil in step 1 and a spoonful of minced sun-dried tomatoes along with the basil in step 6. Replace the chicken broth with vegetable broth (page 192).

SERVING SUGGESTIONS: Follow this soup with a main course of baked, grilled, or roasted chicken, sautéed turkey cutlets, or pork chops.

Overleaf:
Zucchini Soup with
Cheddar Rusks

MUSHROOM BARLEY SOUP

*F*resh white mushrooms are used in this version of a traditional winter soup, but feel free to bolster the flavor by incorporating your favorite fresh or dried wild mushrooms. A dollop of good sherry added at the last moment brings this humble dish up to a whole new level.

MAKES 8 SERVINGS

1	tablespoon vegetable oil	¾	cup pearl barley
1	onion, finely diced	½	teaspoon salt, or to taste
1	carrot, finely diced	½	teaspoon freshly ground black pepper, or to taste
1	celery stalk, finely diced		
1	parsnip, finely diced (optional)	1	tablespoon minced fresh parsley
3	cups sliced white mushrooms	2	tablespoons dry sherry or sherry wine vinegar (optional)
8	cups chicken broth (page 193)		

1. Heat the oil in a soup pot over medium heat. Add the onion and sauté, stirring frequently, for 10 minutes, or until golden brown.

2. Add the carrot, celery, parsnip, and mushrooms. Stir well to combine with the onion; cover the pot and cook over low heat for 3 to 4 minutes.

3. Remove the cover and add the broth and barley. Bring the broth to a boil, then reduce the heat and simmer gently over low heat for 30 minutes, or until the barley is soft to the bite.

4. Add salt and pepper to taste. Stir in the parsley. If desired, add the sherry or vinegar at the last moment. Serve hot.

NUTRITION INFORMATION, PER SERVING (6 OUNCES): 150 calories, 8 grams protein, 4 grams fat, 21 grams carbohydrates, 790 milligrams sodium, 0 milligrams cholesterol.

PREPARATION NOTE: This soup will mellow and deepen in flavor if it is prepared a day ahead. It will also thicken slightly; to adjust the consistency add a little water or additional broth and reheat.

SERVING SUGGESTIONS: This substantial soup makes a good light supper. If you take it on a picnic, preheat a Thermos® by rinsing it with boiling water before filling.

Potato, Escarole, and Country Ham Soup

Country hams have a taste and texture altogether different from that of other hams. They usually are slowly air-cured in smokehouses, which gives them their unique salty, smoky taste. Different parts of the country swear by their own special curing techniques, as well as the way in which their pigs are fed, as the keys to producing the ultimate ham. Ask your deli manager or butcher to help you find a really fine country ham or at least a suitable substitute.

MAKES 6 TO 8 SERVINGS

1	tablespoon unsalted butter	1	sprig fresh thyme
1	onion, diced	2	cups cleaned and chopped escarole
1	leek, white and light green portion,		(about 8 ounces)
	washed and minced	1	cup diced country ham
1	celery stalk, trimmed and diced	½	teaspoon salt, or to taste
2 to 3	garlic cloves, peeled and minced	¼	teaspoon freshly ground black pepper,
4	cups chicken broth (page 193)		or to taste
2	potatoes, peeled and thinly sliced		

1. Heat the butter in a soup pot over low heat; add the onion, leek, celery, and garlic, and stir until they are evenly coated with butter. Cover the pot and cook until tender and translucent, 6 to 8 minutes.

2. Add the broth, potatoes, and thyme. Simmer the soup until the potatoes are beginning to disintegrate, 15 to 20 minutes.

3. Add the escarole and diced ham, and simmer the soup for another 12 to 15 minutes, or until all ingredients are tender.

4. Add salt and generous amounts of pepper to taste, and serve the soup in a heated soup tureen or individual bowls.

NUTRITION INFORMATION, PER SERVING (6 OUNCES): 175 calories, 11 grams protein, 11 grams fat, 5 grams carbohydrates, 370 milligrams sodium, 35 milligrams cholesterol.

VARIATIONS: The ham can be omitted and vegetable broth (page 192) used for a meatless soup.

The soup can be puréed once the potatoes are tender, before adding the shredded escarole and ham.

PREPARATION NOTE: To make the soup in advance, complete the recipe through step 3, then cool to room temperature, transfer to a bowl or container, and refrigerate for up to 3 days or freeze for up to 1 month.

SERVING SUGGESTIONS: Pair this soup with a hearty sandwich for a Sunday supper, or follow it with an omelet.

TORTILLA SOUP

*T*his soup has a rich corn flavor which comes from toasting corn tortillas before cooking them in a rich chicken broth. Blue corn tortillas make an interesting garnish. If you have trouble locating them, try a specialty store or the frozen-food section of a health-food store.

MAKES 10 SERVINGS

6 corn tortillas (6-inch diameter)	1 tablespoon ground cumin
1 tablespoon corn oil	2 teaspoons mild chili powder
3 cloves garlic, finely minced	2 bay leaves
1 yellow onion, finely minced	Salt to taste
4 plum tomatoes, peeled and chopped (page 191), or 1½ cups chopped canned whole tomatoes	Freshly ground black pepper to taste
	1 avocado
8 cups chicken broth (page 193)	2 teaspoons fresh lemon juice
2 tablespoons chopped fresh cilantro	½ cup shredded sharp Cheddar cheese
	½ cup shredded cooked chicken breast

1. Preheat the oven to 350 degrees F. Cut the tortillas into matchstick-thick strips. Place them on an ungreased baking sheet and toast them in the preheated oven until they are crisp and barely golden, about 5 minutes.

2. Heat the corn oil in a soup pot and add the garlic and onion. Sauté over medium heat, stirring frequently, for 10 minutes, or until they are golden brown.

3. Set about ¾ cup of the tortilla strips aside. Add the remaining strips, tomatoes, broth, cilantro, cumin, chili, and bay leaves to the pot. Reduce the heat to low, and simmer the soup for 30 to 40 minutes.

4. Remove and discard the bay leaves. Cool the soup slightly, then purée it in a blender or food processor.

5. Bring the soup back to a simmer just before serving, and adjust the seasoning with salt and pepper to taste.

6. Peel, pit, and dice the avocado; toss with the lemon juice. Garnish each bowl of soup with the cheese, chicken, reserved tortilla strips, and avocado.

NUTRITION INFORMATION, PER SERVING (6 OUNCES): 155 calories, 9 grams protein, 8 grams fat, 12 grams carbohydrates, 668 milligrams sodium, 10 milligrams cholesterol.

VARIATIONS: The avocado can be blended with just enough water or chicken stock to make a smooth purée with the consistency of thin mayonnaise to drizzle onto the soup. Or make a purée of similar consistency with roasted peppers and cream.

SERVING SUGGESTIONS: For a restaurant-type effect, transfer the avocado and/or pepper purée to a squirt bottle, the kind used for ketchup and mustard. Make random patterns or more formal designs on the surface of the soup. To get a marbled effect, make concentric circles, and draw lines through the circles with a knife or skewer.

Double Chicken Broth with Shiitakes, Scallions, and Tofu

*T*he broth you use in this soup must be rich enough to stand on its own. Homemade broth, prepared from a stewing hen, is the best choice.

MAKES 4 TO 6 SERVINGS

¼	pound boneless, skinless chicken breast (about ½ breast)
4	cups chicken broth (page 193)
3 to 4	fresh shiitake mushrooms, stems removed and sliced
3	scallions, sliced on the bias
½	cup diced firm tofu
1	teaspoon peeled and minced fresh gingerroot
1	tablespoon chopped fresh cilantro
2	teaspoons soy or tamari sauce
¼	teaspoon freshly ground black pepper, or to taste
	Freshly squeezed lime juice to taste

1. Trim away any visible fat from the chicken breast and cut the meat into thin strips.
2. Bring the broth to a simmer in a soup pot over high heat. Add the chicken, reduce the heat to low, and simmer for 10 minutes. Skim away any foam that rises to the surface.
3. Add the shiitakes, scallions, tofu, ginger, and cilantro. Simmer gently until all ingredients are heated through and the flavors are blended, about 5 minutes.
4. Add the soy sauce, freshly ground pepper, and lime juice. Serve in heated bowls.

NUTRITION INFORMATION, PER SERVING (6 OUNCES): 180 calories, 4 grams protein, 10 grams fat, 18 grams carbohydrates, 285 milligrams sodium, 40 milligrams cholesterol.

PREPARATION NOTES: For a more substantial one-pot meal, increase the amount of chicken breast and include some of the following: broccoli florets, sliced celery, shredded bok choy or celery cabbage, snow peas, green beans, cooked chickpeas, or cucumbers.

SERVING SUGGESTIONS: This soup would be a good introduction to a meal of stir-fried shrimp and vegetables. Or serve it as an entire meal, ladled over noodles or rice.

Entrées

PHEASANT WITH CRANBERRY PEPPERCORN SAUCE

*T*oday, pheasant, once available mostly in the fall, is one of the most readily available game birds because it now is farm raised. It has a relatively mild flavor and succulent flesh.

MAKES 4 SERVINGS

2	teaspoons cornstarch	¼	cup dry red wine
2	whole pheasants, trussed	2	cups chicken broth (page 193)
½	teaspoon salt, or to taste	1	cup fresh cranberries
¼	teaspoon freshly ground black pepper, or to taste	⅓	cup sugar
		½	teaspoon cracked black peppercorns
2	sprigs fresh parsley or thyme	2	tablespoons ruby port
2	bay leaves	2	tablespoons butter (optional)

1. Preheat the oven to 450 degrees F. Dilute the cornstarch with an equal amount of cold water and set aside.

2. Pat the pheasants dry with paper towels and rub the skin with salt and pepper. Stuff the cavities with the parsley or thyme sprigs and bay leaves.

3. Place the pheasants on a rack in a roasting pan and roast for 55 to 60 minutes, to an internal temperature of 165 degrees F, or until the juices show no traces of pink when the thigh is pierced with a kitchen fork.

4. Remove the pheasants from the roasting pan; set aside and keep warm. Immediately add the wine to the roasting pan. Place the pan over medium-high heat and bring to a boil, stirring; scrape the pan well to release all the browned bits on the bottom. Pour the juices into a saucepan.

5. Add the broth, cranberries, sugar, and cracked peppercorns to the saucepan and simmer over medium heat until the cranberries are very tender, 10 to 12 minutes.

Preceding Page:
Braised Lamb
Shanks with
Creole Vegetables

6. Stir the diluted cornstarch if necessary to recombine and add it to the sauce; simmer for 2 more minutes.

7. Stir the ruby port and butter into the sauce. Add salt to taste. Cut the pheasants in half and serve with the sauce.

NUTRITION INFORMATION, PER SERVING: 450 calories, 46 grams protein, 22 grams fat, 11 grams carbohydrates, 365 milligrams sodium, 150 milligrams cholesterol.

PREPARATION NOTES: Substitute a roasting chicken or turkey breast for the pheasant. For additional flavor, lay strips of prosciutto over the breast.

Dried cranberries can be used instead of fresh or frozen ones. Use ½ cup dried cranberries and plump in port as directed on page 191.

SERVING SUGGESTIONS: A bold, full-bodied wine such as a merlot or petit syrah, would be a nice partner for this dish. Serve wild mushrooms or Wild Rice Patties (page 106) as an accompaniment.

Overleaf:
Asian Vegetables and
Marinated Bean Curd

Asian Vegetables and Marinated Bean Curd

*A*lthough this recipe does call for some last-minute assembly, most of the time-consuming work is done in advance. In fact, the tofu needs to marinate several hours or overnight, so plan ahead.

MAKES 4 SERVINGS

½	pound firm tofu
½	cup tamari or low-sodium soy sauce
3	tablespoons dark sesame oil
¼	cup peanut oil, plus additional for frying
1	scallion, chopped
1	teaspoon minced fresh gingerroot
1	garlic clove, finely minced

1	carrot, julienned or coarsely grated
1	red or green bell pepper, julienned
1	cup peeled, seeded, diced cucumber
1	celery stalk, julienned
1	cup sliced mushrooms
1	cup shredded bok choy
1	recipe Spicy Peanut Noodles (recipe follows)

1. Remove tofu from the package and drain on paper towels for several minutes.

2. Combine the tamari or soy sauce, sesame oil, peanut oil, scallion, ginger, and garlic in a bowl; stir to blend thoroughly.

3. Cut the tofu into 2-inch cubes, add to the marinade, and toss gently to coat evenly. Allow the tofu to marinate for several hours or overnight in the refrigerator.

4. Heat about ⅛ inch of peanut oil in a skillet over high heat.

5. Remove the tofu from the marinade and blot it dry on paper towels; reserve the marinade. Place the tofu in the hot oil and pan-fry until golden brown on all sides, about 5 minutes.

6. Meanwhile, steam or blanch the carrot, pepper, cucumber, celery, mushrooms, and bok choy until wilted. Mound the noodles on a heated platter and top with the vegetables.

7. Set the tofu on paper towels, and drain briefly; place on the steamed vegetables.

8. Serve the tofu accompanied by the reserved marinade to use as a dipping sauce.

NUTRITION INFORMATION, PER SERVING: 525 calories, 19 grams protein, 43 grams fat, 17 grams carbohydrates, 1,225 milligrams sodium, 0 milligrams cholesterol.

VARIATIONS: Serve the vegetables and tofu over a bed of steamed rice or plain noodles, rather than the Spicy Peanut Noodles. Replace the tofu with cooked poultry or shellfish for a nonvegetarian version.

SERVING SUGGESTIONS: Make this dish a part of a more elaborate buffet, and serve it with a variety of raw marinated salads. It can be served warm, at room temperature, or chilled.

SPICY PEANUT NOODLES

Use a "natural" peanut butter, one that contains no added sugars, oils, or preservatives.

MAKES 4 SERVINGS

¼ cup peanut butter	½ teaspoon rice wine
½ cup chicken broth (page 193)	2 garlic cloves, minced
¼ cup soy or tamari sauce	1 tablespoon minced fresh cilantro
1 tablespoon sugar	1 (12-ounce) package lo mein noodles
2 teaspoons hot chili oil	Salt to taste

1. Combine peanut butter, chicken broth, soy sauce, sugar, oil, and rice wine in a bowl and whisk to blend thoroughly.
2. Add the garlic and the cilantro, and stir. Cover and refrigerate for 1 hour.
3. Cook the noodles in a large pot of boiling, salted water until just tender. Drain in a colander, and toss with the peanut sauce.

NUTRITION INFORMATION, PER SERVING: 590 calories, 13 grams protein, 37 grams fat, 58 grams carbohydrates, 855 milligrams sodium, 0 milligrams cholesterol.

VARIATIONS: Replace the peanut butter with tahini paste. Scatter toasted sesame seeds over the dressed noodles.

Substitute spaghetti, cappellini, or any other long pasta for lo mein.

AHEAD OF TIME: This dish can be held in the refrigerator. Undercook the noodles very slightly, drain, rinse in cold water, and toss gently with about 1 tablespoon of light sesame or peanut oil. Reheat the noodles in a pot of simmering water for 2 to 3 minutes, drain thoroughly, and finish the dish.

SAUTÉED VENISON WITH WILD MUSHROOMS AND ZINFANDEL SAUCE

*V*enison is a lean meat, low in fat and cholesterol. Now raised on farms throughout the country, it is relatively easy to find and is a consistently good product. Farm-raised game has the advantage of a more controlled environment as it is raised and butchered.

MAKES 4 SERVINGS

1 teaspoon cornstarch	1 garlic clove, crushed
½ cup zinfandel, or other dry red wine	2 tablespoons minced shallots
4 (5- to 6-ounce) venison steaks	1 tablespoon tomato paste
½ teaspoon salt	1 cup chopped chanterelle mushrooms
¼ teaspoon freshly ground black pepper	½ cup chicken broth (page 193)
¼ cup olive oil	

1. Preheat the oven to 250 degrees F. Dilute the cornstarch in 2 tablespoons of the zinfandel.

2. Trim the steaks of any excess fat; blot them dry with paper towels and season generously with salt and pepper.

3. Heat the oil in a skillet over high heat. Sauté the steaks, turning once, about 6 minutes total for medium-rare.

4. Transfer the steaks to a baking dish and keep them warm in the oven while finishing the sauce.

5. Pour off all but enough oil to leave a light film on the bottom of the skillet. Return the skillet to low heat.

6. Add the garlic and shallots, and sauté, stirring constantly, for 1 minute.

7. Add the tomato paste and sauté, stirring constantly, for 2 more minutes.

8. Add the mushrooms and sauté until they begin to release their juices, about 3 minutes.

9. Add the remaining wine, stirring well to blend the wine and tomato paste, and simmer for another minute.

10. Add the chicken broth, raise the heat slightly to bring to a rapid simmer, and cook for another minute. Add the diluted cornstarch and cook for another minute; season with salt and pepper to taste.

11. Remove the steaks from the oven, place them on plates, and pool the sauce in front of the meat.

NUTRITION INFORMATION, PER SERVING: 380 calories, 48 grams protein, 19 grams fat, 3 grams carbohydrates, 215 milligrams sodium, 175 milligrams cholesterol.

VARIATIONS: Any type of mushroom may be used in place of chanterelles. Fresh sage or rosemary would make a nice addition to the sauce, and a little butter may be added to make it richer and give it a little more body.

SERVING SUGGESTIONS: Oven-roasted garlic potatoes, or Potato Cheddar Casserole (page 104) go well with this dish.

CHICKEN POT PIE

*P*ot pies are familiar comfort food to many people. This tradition draws from the meat pies, "pasties," and turnovers popular from medieval times onward. In fact, pies made with fruit were at first considered somewhat heretical, both in the New World and the Old.

MAKES 4 SERVINGS

¾	pound cooked chicken meat (about 3 cups)	1	potato, peeled and diced
2	tablespoons butter or vegetable oil	½	cup fresh or frozen green peas
3	tablespoons flour		Salt to taste
3	cups chicken broth (page 193)		Freshly ground black pepper to taste
1	onion, diced	2	tablespoons chopped fresh parsley
2	carrots, diced	½	recipe Angel Biscuits (page 164)
1	celery stalk, diced	1	egg yolk
		2	tablespoons milk

1. Trim and dice the chicken and set it aside.

2. Heat the butter or oil in a saucepan. Add the flour and cook over medium heat for 3 minutes, stirring constantly; do not let the flour burn.

3. Gradually add the broth, whisking vigorously to work out any lumps.

4. Bring the broth to a simmer. It will thicken into a sauce as it cooks.

5. Add the onion, carrots, celery, and potato to the sauce, and simmer over very low heat until the vegetables are tender, about 20 minutes.

6. Add the chicken and peas to the vegetables, and remove from the heat. Adjust the seasonings, add the parsley and turn the mixture into a deep baking dish or 4 individual ovenproof crocks.

7. Preheat the oven to 350 degrees F. Roll out the biscuit dough to about ½-inch thickness and cut out 1 large piece or 4 small ones; dough should be just large enough to cover the baking dish or crocks. Cut vents in the dough to allow steam to escape. Cover the dish or crocks with the dough.

8. Mix together the egg yolk and milk, and lightly brush the mixture over the dough. Bake for about 45 minutes, or until the tops are fully baked and golden brown. Serve at once.

NUTRITION INFORMATION, PER SERVING: 535 calories, 38 grams protein, 20 grams fat, 47 grams carbohydrates, 1,030 milligrams sodium, 90 milligrams cholesterol.

VARIATIONS: Other vegetables, including cooked leeks, parsnips, turnips, green beans, rutabagas, or cooked dried beans can be used.

Puff pastry can be used for a more elegant presentation. Or, replace the biscuit topping with a layer of mashed potatoes.

SERVING SUGGESTIONS: This is a meal in a single dish, and the only accompaniment you may want is a simple green salad or a side dish of Pickled Beets and Onions (page 139).

*T*his "roll-your-own" meal is a favorite for easy entertaining. Put all the garnishes and condiments out in pretty bowls and relax.

MAKES 4 SERVINGS

4	(4- to 5-ounce) boneless, skinless chicken breasts	1	cup shredded Cheddar or Monterey Jack cheese
1	tablespoon olive oil	1	cup shredded iceberg lettuce
2	tablespoons fresh lemon juice	1	cup diced tomatoes
	Salt to taste	½	cup sour cream
	Freshly ground black pepper to taste	½	cup sliced scallions
½	teaspoon ground cumin	¼	cup chopped cilantro
	Salsa (page 123)	8	flour tortillas
	Guacamole (page 127)		

1. Trim the chicken breasts and pat them dry.

2. Combine the olive oil, lemon juice, salt, pepper, and cumin in a shallow dish. Add the chicken breasts and turn to coat evenly; marinate in the refrigerator for 30 to 45 minutes.

3. While the chicken is marinating, prepare a charcoal grill. When the coals are hot, grill the chicken until it is cooked through, turning occasionally, 7 to 8 minutes.

4. Assemble all of the other ingredients.

5. Heat the flour tortillas by steaming them over a little simmering water, or by wrapping them in foil and heating them on the grill as the chicken cooks.

6. Remove the chicken from the grill and slice it into diagonal strips on the bias.

7. Serve the chicken on a platter with the garnishes and heated tortillas.

NUTRITION INFORMATION, PER SERVING: 675 calories, 47 grams protein, 65 grams fat, 65 grams carbohydrates, 1,080 milligrams sodium, 115 milligrams cholesterol.

VARIATIONS: The chicken may be sautéed instead of grilled. Heat about 2 tablespoons of oil in a skillet over high heat. Cut the chicken into strips before sautéing, and add them to the hot oil. Sauté, stirring frequently, until the chicken is fully cooked, 3 to 5 minutes. Sliced or diced red onion, black olives, or diced avocado may be substituted or added.

ROASTED EGGPLANT CALZONE

Roasting eggplant in the oven or over hot coals gives it a rich smoky taste.

MAKES 4 SERVING

1	recipe Basic Flatbread dough (page 152), divided into 4 equal balls
	Cornmeal for sprinkling pans
1	eggplant (¾ to 1 pound), sliced crosswise
¼	cup olive oil
½	teaspoon salt, or to taste
¼	teaspoon freshly ground black pepper, or to taste
1	clove garlic, crushed
1	cup sliced white mushrooms
¼	cup minced onion
2	cups fresh spinach leaves, washed thoroughly and stems removed
1	cup part-skim ricotta cheese
⅓	cup freshly grated Parmesan cheese
¼	cup minced fresh basil
1	egg, lightly beaten
¼	teaspoon crushed red pepper flakes, or to taste
	Tomato-Ginger Coulis (page 134)

1. Preheat the oven to 425 degrees F. Cover the dough with a kitchen towel, and let it rise in a warm place for about 45 minutes. Sprinkle about 2 tablespoons of cornmeal on 2 baking sheets, baking stones, or pizza stones.

2. Meanwhile, brush the eggplant slices on both sides with some of the olive oil, season well with salt and pepper, and place on a clean baking sheet. Roast in the preheated oven until very tender, about 20 minutes. Cut the eggplant into narrow strips or large dice and set aside.

3. In a skillet, sauté the garlic, mushrooms, and onion in 2 tablespoons of the olive oil over medium heat until soft and the onions are translucent, about 5 minutes. Transfer to a mixing bowl and cool slightly.

4. Return the skillet to high heat, add another tablespoon of olive oil, and add the spinach. Cover the skillet and cook until the spinach is wilted and tender, 2 to 3 minutes. Drain the spinach in a colander, then chop coarsely and add to the mushrooms and onion. Add the ricotta, Parmesan cheese, basil, egg, red pepper, and salt and pepper to taste to the mushroom and spinach mixture. Blend well.

5. Roll or stretch the dough into 6-inch circles. Divide the ricotta mixture equally onto one-half of each disk, leaving a 1-inch border. Top with eggplant. Fold the untopped portion of

the dough over the filling and pinch the edges together to seal. Crimp or use the tines of a fork dipped in warm water to help seal the dough.

6. Place the calzones on the prepared baking sheets or stones and bake in the preheated oven for 25 to 30 minutes or until the crust is golden brown. Serve immediately with Tomato-Ginger Coulis on the side.

NUTRITION INFORMATION, PER SERVING: 1,157 calories, 44 grams protein, 37 grams fat, 167 grams carbohydrates, 1,177 milligrams sodium, 113 milligrams cholesterol.

VARIATIONS: Add a variety of grilled or roasted vegetables such as zucchini, red peppers, tomatoes, or sweet potatoes to this filling. Replace part of the ricotta cheese (up to 3 ounces) with crumbled feta or goat cheese.

AHEAD OF TIME: The filling can be held for up to 2 days in the refrigerator; the filled calzones can be held for several hours before baking. Return them to room temperature for about 1 hour before baking.

SERVING SUGGESTIONS: A fresh tomato sauce or a classic marinara can be served in place of the coulis. Heat the sauce and serve it in individual cups, or ladle some directly over each calzone. A peppery red wine such as a zinfandel or merlot would be a fine accompaniment.

CIA Club Sandwich

*T*his recipe takes a few liberties with the classic coffee shop favorite, turning it into a party-size sandwich for four. If you prefer a more traditional look, substitute good white bread with a firm texture.

MAKES 4 SERVINGS

1 small round country-style loaf of bread	4 strips bacon, cooked crisp and drained
Vegetable oil as needed	4 leaves green leaf or iceberg lettuce
½ cup mayonnaise, or as needed	Salt to taste
½ pound thinly sliced ham	Freshly ground black pepper to taste
1 ripe tomato, thinly sliced	
½ pound thinly sliced cooked turkey breast	

1. Slice the bread horizontally to make 3 layers. Brush each layer with oil and toast, grill, or broil lightly.

2. Spread a slice of the toasted bread with mayonnaise and arrange the ham and tomatoes evenly over it.

3. Add another slice of bread, spread with mayonnaise, and top with the turkey, bacon strips, and lettuce. Season well with salt and pepper if desired.

4. Spread the last slice of bread with a little more mayonnaise, and place it on top, mayonnaise side down.

5. Secure the sandwich with picks, and cut into 4 quarters.

NUTRITION INFORMATION, PER SERVING: 380 calories, 8 grams protein, 17 grams fat, 26 grams carbohydrates, 250 milligrams sodium, 26 milligrams cholesterol.

PREPARATION NOTES: The ingredients can be assembled in advance, but for the best results, toast the bread and put the sandwich together as close as possible to serving time.

SERVING SUGGESTIONS: Make this part of a sandwich buffet, and serve a collection of salads—potato, macaroni, or pasta; Warm Black-eyed Pea Salad (page 10); tossed greens; or marinated vegetables—along with crisp Half-Sour Pickles (page 138). Beer, iced tea, lemonade, or soft drinks all are appropriate.

An American Bounty

GRILLED DUCK BREAST

Roasting a whole duck is a lengthy (and sometimes smoky and messy) process. When you grill just the breast, cooking time is greatly reduced. Ask your butcher for just breasts, or have a whole duck cut into pieces and save the legs to braise another day.

MAKES 4 SERVINGS

2 whole skinless and boneless duck breasts	1-inch piece fresh gingerroot, thinly sliced
⅓ cup soy sauce	2 teaspoons dark sesame oil
⅓ cup water	½ teaspoon cracked black peppercorns

1. Cut the duck breasts in half and pat dry.

2. Combine the remaining ingredients in a shallow bowl or baking dish and mix well. Add the duck breasts and turn them to coat evenly. Cover the dish and place it in the refrigerator for at least 1 hour, or as long as overnight.

3. Preheat a grill: Gas grills should be set on medium-high; charcoal should be glowing red with a coating of white ash. Rub the grill lightly with oil on a cloth or with a brush.

4. Remove the duck from the marinade, pulling it along the rim of the dish to remove any excess marinade. Place the duck on the grill and cook, turning once, for a total of 8 to 10 minutes for medium rare, 12 to 15 for well done. Serve at once.

NUTRITION INFORMATION, PER SERVING: 260 calories, 28 grams protein, 15 grams fat, 3 grams carbohydrates, 1,483 milligrams sodium, 99 milligrams cholesterol.

SERVING SUGGESTIONS: Grilled vegetables and Pasta with Sautéed Country Ham, Apples, and Hazelnuts (page 38) are good side dishes with this.

For a cold supper, grill the duck in advance and let it cool, but do not refrigerate. Slice it thinly, and fan or mound it on a bed of mixed greens. Top with chopped roasted peanuts and sliced scallions, and dress with any of the vinaigrettes (pages 14–15).

MAPLE-SOY GLAZED TROUT

his recipe calls for pan-dressed trout—trout that has been gutted, scaled, trimmed, and cleaned. Typically, the head and tail would be left on, but have them removed if you prefer.

MAKES 4 SERVINGS

4	pan-dressed trout	1	tablespoon vegetable oil
½	teaspoon salt	¼	cup maple syrup
¼	teaspoon freshly ground black pepper	4	teaspoons soy sauce
⅓	cup all-purpose flour	4	teaspoons toasted sesame seeds
1½	teaspoons unsalted butter		(page 192)

1. Rinse the trout well in cold water, rub the cavity to remove traces of blood, and pat dry.
2. Combine the salt, pepper, and flour in a shallow pan. Dredge the trout in the flour and shake off any excess.
3. Heat the butter and oil in a skillet over high heat until very hot. Add the trout and reduce the heat to medium. Sauté without moving on the first side for about 4 minutes, or until the skin is golden brown. Turn the fish once and finish cooking on the second side for another 3 to 4 minutes.
4. Remove the trout from the skillet and keep it warm. Add the maple syrup and soy sauce to the pan. Increase the heat to high and reduce the mixture until thickened, about 2 minutes.
5. Return the trout to the skillet and turn to coat evenly with the maple-soy glaze. Place the trout on a heated platter and sprinkle with the toasted sesame seeds.

NUTRITION INFORMATION, PER SERVING: 240 calories, 19 grams protein, 9 grams fat, 22 grams carbohydrates, 430 milligrams sodium, 50 milligrams cholesterol.

PREPARATION NOTES: Replacing regular soy sauce with a reduced-sodium version will cut the total sodium in this dish by about one-third.

VARIATION: Use other small fish (perch, coho salmon, or mackerel) instead of trout.

SERVING SUGGESTIONS: Garlic Cheese Grits Casserole (page 109), home fries, or barley pilaf would be nice with this for breakfast, lunch, or dinner.

PAN-FRIED HAM STEAK WITH RED-EYE GRAVY

*T*his traditional Southern breakfast is best made with country-style cured ham. If you are able to find such a ham in your area, you may want to blanch the steaks to remove any excess salt.

MAKES 4 SERVINGS

4	ham steaks, ¼ inch thick
¼	cup very cold water
¼	cup very strong coffee

1. Place the ham steaks in a cast-iron skillet over medium heat.
2. Cook the steaks, turning occasionally, until any fat is very crisp and the steaks take on a dark glaze, 12 to 15 minutes.
3. Transfer the steaks to warmed plates or a platter.
4. Pour off any excess fat from the skillet and return to medium heat. Add the cold water to the skillet, stirring and scraping the pan to release and dissolve the drippings.
5. Add the coffee, and reduce the gravy slightly over medium heat.
6. Pour the gravy over the steaks and serve at once.

NUTRITION INFORMATION, PER SERVING: 340 calories, 30 grams protein, 24 grams fat, trace of carbohydrates, 1,660 milligrams sodium, 85 milligrams cholesterol.

PREPARATION NOTES: To blanch country-cured ham steaks, place them in a skillet and add enough cold water to cover generously. Bring to a simmer over low heat, simmer for 2 or 3 minutes, then drain and pat dry before continuing with the recipe.

SERVING SUGGESTIONS: The classic accompaniments are grits and biscuits. The gravy is typically poured over the steak and grits, and served with biscuits.

HALIBUT STEAK WITH LIME BUTTER

*H*alibut has a snowy-white flesh with a firm texture and a sweet, fresh taste. Pairing it with a crisp cashew crust and a piquant lime-butter sauce makes for a winning combination.

MAKES 4 SERVINGS

4 halibut steaks, 5 to 6 ounces each	½ cup all-purpose flour
½ teaspoon salt, or to taste	½ cup buttermilk
½ teaspoon coarsely ground black pepper, or to taste	1 cup vegetable oil
¾ cup unsalted toasted cashews (page 192)	3 tablespoons unsalted butter
	2 tablespoons freshly squeezed lime juice
	2 tablespoons minced fresh chives

1. Pat the halibut steaks dry with paper towels and season them with salt and pepper.

2. Combine ½ cup of the cashews with the flour in a food processor or blender; process until the mixture has the consistency of cornmeal.

3. Place the flour mixture in a shallow bowl. Pour the buttermilk into a shallow bowl.

4. Dip the halibut steaks into the buttermilk, drain off the excess, and dip into the flour.

5. Heat about ⅓ inch of vegetable oil in a large skillet over high heat. Carefully add the fish to the hot oil. Cook on the first side for 2 to 3 minutes, or until light, golden brown. Turn the fish once, and cook on the second side, 2 to 3 minutes more, over medium heat.

6. Remove the fish and drain on paper towels. Transfer to a heated serving platter or individual plates; set aside in a warm spot.

7. Pour the oil from the skillet, wipe it out to remove any particles, and return it to high heat.

8. Add butter to the skillet, swirling it in the pan until it begins to turn light brown and has a rich, nutty aroma. Add the lime juice, chives, and the remaining ¼ cup cashews. Continue to swirl the pan over the heat 15 to 20 seconds longer; drizzle the sauce over the fish.

NUTRITION INFORMATION, PER SERVING: 557 calories, 39 grams protein, 35 grams fat, 21 grams carbohydrates, 390 milligrams sodium, 75 milligrams cholesterol.

LOWER-FAT VERSION: Mix ¾ cup bread crumbs and ¼ cup cashews. Dip the fish in buttermilk, top with the bread crumb mixture, and bake at 375 degrees F for 12 minutes. Replace the butter sauce with lemon or lime juice and serve with salsa on the side.

ROAST GAME HENS WITH CORN BREAD STUFFING

*H*ere is a twist on the classic Sunday dinner, with a "Southwestern" appeal.

MAKES 4 SERVINGS

2	game hens, trimmed of all extra fat
1	lemon, thickly sliced
2	garlic cloves, split
	Salt to taste
	Freshly ground black pepper to taste
1	tablespoon vegetable oil
1	onion, diced
1	leek, white part only, diced (optional)
1	celery stalk, diced
1	carrot, diced

2½	cups chicken broth (or as needed) (page 193)
3	tablespoons plumped raisins (page 191)
2	tablespoons chopped fresh parsley
2	cups cubed corn bread
½	cup corn kernels (fresh or frozen)
1	plum tomato, peeled, seeded, and diced (page 191)
2	teaspoons cornstarch, diluted in a little cold water (optional)

1. Rinse the game hens with cool water, pat dry, and rub well with lemon and garlic. Season with salt and pepper.

2. Heat the oil in a skillet over medium heat. Add the onion, leek, celery, and carrot, and cook, stirring until the vegetables are evenly coated with oil. Cover the skillet and continue to cook over low heat for about 10 to 12 minutes.

3. Remove the cover, add ½ cup of the broth and the raisins and parsley; simmer for 5 minutes.

4. Remove the skillet from the heat and add the corn bread; stir to combine and moisten the corn bread. Transfer the corn bread stuffing to a shallow dish, spread it in an even layer, and let it cool to room temperature. Preheat the oven to 350 degrees F.

5. Spoon the cooled stuffing into the birds; fill them but do not pack tightly.

6. Set the birds on a rack in a roasting pan or dish, add about ½ inch of water to the pan, and cover loosely with foil, tenting the hens.

7. Roast the hens in the preheated oven for about 1 hour, to an internal temperature of 165 degrees F, or until the juices released when the thigh is pierced run clear.

8. Transfer the hens to a platter, cover loosely with foil, and keep warm while preparing the sauce.

9. Place the roasting pan over medium heat and bring the contents to a simmer. Carefully skim off as much of the fat as possible. Allow the liquid to reduce slightly, then add the corn and diced tomato; simmer for 10 minutes. Add the diluted cornstarch to thicken the sauce and season to taste with salt and pepper.

10. Carve the hens into pieces and serve with the sauce.

NUTRITION INFORMATION, PER SERVING: 380 calories, 42 grams protein, 9 grams fat, 30 grams carbohydrates, 775 milligrams sodium, 135 milligrams cholesterol.

VARIATION: Add the corn and tomatoes to the stuffing mixture and instead of stuffing the birds with it, use it as a bed for them as they roast.

The stuffing can be used for a 5- to 6-pound roasting chicken. Increase the roasting time by about 40 minutes.

SERVING SUGGESTIONS: Serve this with Chayote Jícama Salsa (page 125). Follow with Triple Chocolate Pecan Brownies (page 169) or Gingercake (page 190).

MUSTARD-FRIED CHICKEN

*H*ere is just one of many versions of an American favorite. Marinating the chicken in a blend of buttermilk, mustard, and tarragon gives it a delicious flavor.

MAKES 6 SERVINGS

2 frying chickens, cut into 8 pieces each	1 teaspoon salt
2 cups buttermilk	½ teaspoon freshly ground black pepper
¼ cup Dijon-style mustard	2 cups all-purpose flour
1 teaspoon chopped fresh tarragon	2 cups vegetable oil

1. Rinse the chicken in cool water and pat dry.

2. Blend the buttermilk, mustard, tarragon, salt, and pepper in a large bowl. Add the chicken pieces, turn to coat them evenly, and let them marinate for 2 to 3 hours, or overnight in the refrigerator.

3. Remove the chicken from the marinade and let it drain briefly. Roll it in the flour, and transfer to a baking sheet. Set aside for about 30 minutes.

4. Preheat the oven to 350 degrees F. Heat about ½ inch of oil in a cast-iron or other deep-sided, heavy-gauge skillet over medium heat. When the oil is hot, but not smoking, add the chicken pieces, a few at a time. Pan-fry, turning to cook all sides, until the chicken is well-browned, a total of 6 to 8 minutes.

5. As the chicken is browned, transfer it to a baking sheet. Bake the chicken pieces in the oven for 30 to 40 minutes, until they are fully cooked (when the thigh is pierced, the juices should run clear).

6. Blot the chicken briefly on paper towels and serve at once.

NUTRITION INFORMATION, PER SERVING: 595 calories, 48 grams protein, 36 grams fat, 20 grams carbohydrates, 410 milligrams sodium, 140 milligrams cholesterol.

SERVING SUGGESTIONS: Coleslaw (page 6) is great with fried chicken. Corn bread or corn sticks are also good while iced tea, lemonade, or cold beer are the natural beverage selections.

Overleaf:
Shaker-style
Stuffed Flank
Steak

SHAKER-STYLE STUFFED FLANK STEAK

*T*he Shakers were one of the many religious groups that fled England for a new world, free from religious persecution. They were famous for their use of herbs, spices, and other flavorings, as well as for their simple life-style and furniture. Shaker recipes often have long ingredient lists, because so many herbs are included to achieve highly prized flavors, but that should not make them daunting.

MAKES 8 SERVINGS

3	tablespoons butter
2	cups bread cubes
1	onion, diced
1	celery stalk, diced
1	cup sliced mushrooms
1	carrot, diced
3	tablespoons chopped mixed fresh herbs, such as chives, parsley, tarragon, chervil, marjoram, thyme, and/or oregano
1/4	pound lean ground beef
1	whole egg
1	flank steak (2 to 3 pounds), butterflied and lightly pounded
1/2	teaspoon salt, or to taste

1/2	teaspoon freshly ground black pepper, or to taste
2	tablespoons vegetable oil

FOR THE SAUCE:

1/2	cup diced onion
1/4	cup diced parsnip (optional)
1/4	cup diced celery
2	tablespoons tomato paste
1/4	cup dry red wine
2	cups beef broth
1	sprig fresh thyme, tarragon, or parsley
1	bay leaf
2	teaspoons cornstarch, diluted in wine or water (optional)
1 to 2	teaspoons balsamic vinegar (optional)

1. Heat 1 tablespoon of the butter in a sauté pan over medium heat. Add the bread cubes and sauté them for 3 to 4 minutes until they take on a light golden color. Transfer the bread cubes to a bowl.

2. Return the sauté pan to medium heat, and melt the remaining 2 tablespoons butter. Add the onion, celery, mushrooms, and carrot, and sauté, stirring frequently, until the onions are translucent, but not brown, about 5 to 6 minutes. Add the vegetables to the bread cubes, and let them cool to room temperature.

3. When the bread and vegetable mixture has cooled, add the herbs, ground meat, and egg. Mix well with a wooden spoon until a relatively homogenous stuffing is formed.

4. Pat the flank steak dry with paper towels, season both sides with salt and pepper, and lay the steak out flat on a work surface.

5. Spread the stuffing evenly over the opened flank steak. Roll the steak up, completely enclosing the stuffing. Tie the steak with butcher's twine at 2-inch intervals.

6. Heat the oil in a Dutch oven or large skillet over high heat. Add the steak and sear on all sides to a deep brown, 8 to 10 minutes. Remove the steak.

7. Add the onion, parsnip, and celery to the skillet, and sauté, stirring frequently, over medium heat until the onion just begins to turn brown, 10 to 12 minutes. Add the tomato paste and sauté, stirring constantly, for 2 more minutes.

8. Add the wine to the skillet, stirring well to release any drippings sticking to the pan, and reduce by one-half. Add the broth, thyme, and bay leaf, and bring to a simmer.

9. Return the steak to the pan, cover the skillet, and cook over low heat or in a 325-degree F oven for about 1½ hours, or until the meat is fork tender.

10. Transfer the steak to a heated platter, moisten with some of the cooking liquid, and cover loosely. Set aside in a warm spot while completing the sauce.

11. Place the skillet over high heat and bring the liquid to a full boil. Skim any fat from the surface, and reduce the heat slightly to a brisk simmer. Reduce the sauce to about 2 cups.

12. Add the diluted cornstarch to the sauce; taste and correct the seasonings as desired with more herbs, salt, pepper, or a dash of red wine or balsamic vinegar.

13. Cut the string away from the steak and carve it into ¾-inch-thick slices. Ladle some of the sauce over the meat and pass the rest at the table.

NUTRITION INFORMATION, PER SERVING: 399 calories, 49 grams protein, 19 grams fat, 5 grams carbohydrates, 455 milligrams sodium, 175 milligrams cholesterol.

AHEAD OF TIME: Like many braised dishes, this flank steak seems to get better after resting overnight in the refrigerator. Stop after step 9, let the steak and the sauce cool to room temperature, and then cover and refrigerate.

SERVING SUGGESTIONS: Plain egg noodles make an excellent vehicle for the savory sauce. Add a steamed or boiled green vegetable and follow with Shaker Lemon Pie (page 178).

Corn Cake with Tomato-Leek Sauce

*C*ornmeal is available in three grinds: fine, medium (the type most generally found in grocery stores), and coarse. The coarse meal is generally preferred for polenta and may be found in gourmet shops and larger supermarkets.

MAKES 4 SERVINGS

2   leeks
5   cups water
1   teaspoon salt, or to taste
1¼ cups coarsely ground yellow cornmeal
¼   teaspoon freshly ground black pepper, or to taste
2   tablespoons extra-virgin olive oil
3   garlic cloves, minced
¼   pound mushrooms, sliced
2   plum tomatoes, peeled, seeded, and chopped (page 191)

1   cup chicken broth (page 193) or vegetable broth (page 192)
1   cup port wine
2   teaspoons shredded fresh sage
2   teaspoons chopped fresh thyme
¼   cup julienned sun-dried tomatoes, reconstituted if necessary (page 191)
¼   cup freshly grated dry Monterey Jack or Parmesan cheese

1. Lightly oil an 8-inch round cake pan. Trim and split or quarter the leeks lengthwise and slice the light green and white parts crosswise, about ¼ inch thick. Place in a strainer and rinse thoroughly to remove all traces of dirt.

2. Bring the water to a rolling boil in a sauce pot over high heat. Add the salt. Whisking constantly, add the cornmeal in a very thin stream.

3. Allow the liquid to return to a boil, still stirring constantly, then reduce the heat to low. Simmer the cornmeal, stirring frequently, for about 40 minutes. The cornmeal is properly cooked when it forms a smooth heavy mass that pulls cleanly away from the sides of the pot. Add salt and pepper to taste.

4. Pour the cooked cornmeal into the prepared cake pan and spread it into an even layer. After it has cooled to room temperature, tightly cover the pan with aluminum foil and refrigerate for at least 8 hours.

5. Heat the olive oil in a skillet over high heat. Add the garlic, leeks, and mushrooms, and sauté, stirring frequently, until the leeks are translucent and tender, 6 to 8 minutes.

6. Preheat the oven to 400 degrees F.

7. Add the tomatoes to the skillet and continue to sauté just until any moisture from the tomatoes cooks away, about 2 minutes.

8. Add the broth and the port wine, and simmer over low heat for 15 to 20 minutes.

9. Meanwhile, uncover the corn cake and sprinkle the sage, thyme, sun-dried tomatoes, and cheese over the top. Replace the foil loosely and bake for 12 minutes; remove the foil and bake another 5 minutes or until the cheese is lightly browned. Cut the cake into 4 wedges.

10. Adjust the seasoning of the sauce if necessary with salt, pepper, or a dash of lemon juice. Pool the sauce on a heated serving platter or individual plates and top with the wedges.

NUTRITION INFORMATION, PER SERVING (¼ OF CAKE): 377 calories, 13 grams protein, 17 grams fat, 45 grams carbohydrates, 500 milligrams sodium, 25 milligrams cholesterol.

VARIATIONS: Instead of dry Jack cheese, add crumbled feta and Greek olives. Drizzle the cake with good olive oil and sprinkle with fresh oregano.

SERVING SUGGESTIONS: This is delicious with game, such as rabbit, venison, duck, or goose, or with grilled sausages. For a meatless meal, add a side dish of dark leafy greens or the vegetarian version of Kale with Hot Bacon Vinaigrette (page 116) and Braised Black Beans (page 112), omitting the chorizo sausage.

ROAST TURKEY AND STUFFING

Opt for a turkey that weighs more than 12 pounds because a larger bird gives a greater ratio of meat to bone and thus a better overall yield. Fresh and free-range turkeys are worth seeking out—the difference in flavor is significant.

MAKES ABOUT 10 SERVINGS

1	whole turkey, 14 to 16 pounds	1	carrot, diced
	Salt to taste	1	celery stalk, diced
	Freshly ground black pepper to taste	1	parsnip, diced (optional)
1	recipe stuffing (recipes follow)	4	cups chicken broth (page 193)
4	tablespoons softened butter	1	tablespoon cornstarch
1	onion, diced		

1. Preheat the oven to 350 degrees F.

2. Remove and reserve the giblets (neck, gizzard, and heart) from the turkey. Rinse and pat the turkey dry, inside and out; season well with salt and pepper.

3. Loosely fill the chest and neck cavity with the stuffing. Dot the bird with butter.

4. Place the turkey on a rack in a roasting pan, add about ½ inch of water to the pan, and cover the bird loosely with foil. Roast in the preheated oven for 3 to 4 hours. Add the diced vegetables to the bottom of the roasting pan, and roast the bird for another 1 to 2 hours, or until done. To check for doneness, insert an instant-reading thermometer in the thickest portion of the thigh; it should register 165 degrees F.

5. While the bird is roasting, simmer the giblets in the broth over low heat for 1 hour. Strain the broth and set aside.

6. When the bird is done, remove it from the pan and let it rest on a platter for 15 minutes.

7. To prepare the gravy, pour the pan drippings and vegetables into a saucepan. Pour some of the giblet broth into the roasting pan to dissolve any browned bits clinging to the bottom; add these to the saucepan. Skim as much fat as possible from the surface of the drippings mixture. Add the remaining giblet broth to the saucepan and bring to a simmer over medium heat.

8. Dilute the cornstarch in a little cold water. Add the mixture to the simmering gravy, and simmer for 2 to 3 minutes, or until the gravy thickens. Adjust the seasonings to taste and strain.

9. Spoon the stuffing out of the cavity, carve the turkey, and serve with the pan gravy.

NUTRITION INFORMATION, PER SERVING (TURKEY WITH GRAVY): 350 calories, 52 grams protein, 14 grams fat, 2 grams carbohydrates, 540 milligrams sodium, 140 milligrams cholesterol.

PREPARATION NOTES: The stuffing can be cooked separately in a shallow baking dish, covered with foil. Bake it for about 45 minutes in a 350-degree F oven.

SERVING SUGGESTIONS: Most families have established traditions for Thanksgiving dinners, but to expand your repertoire or add a new dish, try the following: Winter Squashes with Dried Cranberries and Toasted Pecans (page 105), Garlic-Rosemary Potatoes (page 108), Braised Fennel (page 113) and, for dessert, Pumpkin Bread Pudding (page 168).

SAUSAGE AND APPLE STUFFING

MAKES ABOUT 8 CUPS

6 cups cubed white bread	½ cup chopped walnuts, toasted
1 cup hot or mild raw sausage meat, crumbled	(page 192)
	Chicken broth (page 193), as needed
6 tablespoons butter	2 tablespoons minced fresh parsley
½ cup finely diced celery	Salt to taste
½ cup finely diced onion	Freshly ground black pepper to taste
1 cup peeled, cored, and diced raw apples	

1. Preheat the oven to 300 degrees F. Place the cubes on baking sheets and toast lightly, 10 to 12 minutes. They should be slightly dry, but not browned; transfer to a large mixing bowl.
2. Sauté the sausage in a skillet over medium heat until the sausage is cooked through, 5 to 6 minutes. Remove the sausage and drain thoroughly on paper towels to remove excess fat.
3. Return the skillet to medium heat and melt the butter. Add the celery and onion and sauté, stirring frequently, until tender. Combine the sausage, bread cubes, and vegetable mixture.
4. Add the apples and walnuts, and toss to combine. If the stuffing needs additional moisture, add chicken broth—it should be moist enough to hold together when lightly pressed, but not so wet that it packs tightly. Season with parsley and salt and pepper to taste.

NUTRITION INFORMATION, PER SERVING (½ CUP): 230 calories, 5 grams protein, 18 grams fat, 13 grams carbohydrates, 290 milligrams sodium, 60 milligrams cholesterol.

(continues on page 98)

Overleaf:
Roast Turkey
and Stuffing

CHESTNUT AND RAISIN STUFFING

MAKES ABOUT 8 CUPS

6	cups cubed white bread	1	cup raisins, plumped in brandy (page 191)
6	tablespoons butter		
½	cup finely diced celery	¼	cup brandy
½	cup finely diced onion		Chicken broth (page 193), as needed
2	cups coarsely chopped, peeled chestnuts (page 42)		Salt to taste
			Freshly ground black pepper to taste

1. Preheat the oven to 300 degrees F. Place the bread cubes on baking sheets and toast them lightly, 10 to 12 minutes. The bread should be slightly dry, but not browned; transfer the toasted cubes to a large mixing bowl.

2. Melt the butter in a large skillet over medium heat. Add the celery and onion, and sauté, stirring frequently, until tender, about 10 minutes.

3. Add the chestnuts and sauté for 2 more minutes. Add the raisins and brandy, and sauté for about 1 minute, to evaporate the brandy.

4. Add the chestnut mixture to the bread cubes and toss to combine. If necessary, moisten the stuffing with chicken broth—it should be moist enough to hold together when lightly pressed, but not so wet it packs tightly. Season to taste with salt and pepper.

NUTRITION INFORMATION, PER SERVING (½ CUP): 260 calories, trace of protein, 8 grams fat, 43 grams carbohydrates, 200 milligrams sodium, 20 milligrams cholesterol.

PREPARATION NOTE: Chestnuts can be found peeled and frozen from time to time which will greatly reduce the work involved in preparing this stuffing.

An American Bounty

OYSTER AND SPINACH STUFFING

6	cups cubed white bread			Chicken broth (page 193), as needed
6	tablespoons butter		2	tablespoons minced fresh parsley
½	cup finely diced celery			Salt to taste
½	cup finely diced onion			Freshly ground black pepper to taste
3	cups fresh oysters, with their liquor			
1	cup cooked chopped spinach, well drained			

1. Preheat the oven to 300 degrees F. Place the bread cubes on baking sheets and toast them lightly, 10 to 12 minutes. The bread should be slightly dry, but not browned; transfer the toasted cubes to a large mixing bowl.

2. Melt the butter in a large skillet over medium heat. Add the celery and onion, and sauté, stirring frequently, until tender, about 10 minutes.

3. Add the oysters and their liquor, and sauté for 2 more minutes. Add the spinach and sauté for another minute.

4. Add the oyster-spinach mixture to the bread cubes and toss to combine. If necessary, moisten the stuffing with chicken broth—it should be moist enough to hold together when lightly pressed, but not so wet that it packs tightly. Season with parsley and salt and pepper to taste.

NUTRITION INFORMATION, PER SERVING (½ CUP): 165 calories, 8 grams protein, 9 grams fat, 13 grams carbohydrates, 290 milligrams sodium, 60 milligrams cholesterol.

PREPARATION NOTE: For the best results, squeeze the spinach in a piece of cheesecloth, clean dish towel, or paper towels to remove excess water. This can be done before or after chopping.

BRAISED LAMB SHANKS WITH CREOLE VEGETABLES

This dish is also known as Lamb Shanks Pontchartrain, for the lake that is located in southeast Louisianna, just north of New Orleans. The bridge over Lake Ponchartrain is more than 20 miles long, one of the longest in the world.

MAKES 6 SERVINGS

6	lamb shanks (about 1 pound each)
	Salt to taste
	Freshly ground black pepper to taste
2	tablespoons oil, or as needed
1	onion, diced
1	carrot, thinly sliced
1	celery stalk, thinly sliced

½	cup chopped tomatoes (fresh or canned), peeled and seeded (page 191)
4	cups chicken broth (page 193)
1	bay leaf
1	sprig fresh thyme, or ½ teaspoon dried leaves
	Creole Vegetables (page 114)

1. Trim any excess fat from the lamb shanks. Season them with salt and pepper. Heat the oil in a Dutch oven or large skillet over medium-high heat. Add the lamb shanks and sear on all sides to a deep brown, 8 to 10 minutes total. Remove the shanks from the skillet.

2. Add the onion, carrot, and celery to the skillet, and sauté until tender, about 5 minutes.

3. Add the tomatoes and broth, and simmer to reduce slightly, about 5 minutes.

4. Return the shanks to the skillet and add the bay leaf and thyme. Let the shanks simmer, covered, for about 2½ hours, or until the meat is tender enough to be pulled apart with a fork.

5. Adjust the seasoning with salt and pepper and serve with Creole Vegetables.

NUTRITION INFORMATION, PER SERVING: 350 calories, 17 grams protein, 12 grams fat, 50 grams carbohydrates, 500 milligrams sodium, 15 milligrams cholesterol.

SERVING SUGGESTIONS: A dish of Praline Ice Cream (page 173) and steaming black coffee make a fitting conclusion to this meal.

Side Dishes

SAUTÉED ASPARAGUS WITH FRESH MUSHROOMS AND TOASTED PISTACHIOS

$\mathcal{I}$n many areas of the country, morels come into season about the same time that locally grown asparagus appears. This recipe makes the most of these short-lived springtime delicacies.

MAKES 4 SERVINGS

¼	pound fresh morels, or other wild mushrooms	2	tablespoons dry white wine (optional)
20	asparagus medium-thick to thick spears	½	cup heavy cream
2	teaspoons butter	½	teaspoon salt, or to taste
2	teaspoons minced shallots or onions	¼	teaspoon freshly ground black pepper, or to taste
1	leek, trimmed and julienned	¼	cup shelled toasted pistachios (page 192)

1. Wipe the caps of the morels with paper towels and trim the stems. Leave small morels whole; halve or quarter larger caps.

2. Trim the woody stems from the asparagus by bending each stalk until the end breaks off. Peel the remaining lower two-thirds lightly.

3. Heat the butter in a skillet over medium heat and add the shallots, leek, and mushrooms. Sauté, stirring occasionally, until the leek is limp and just starting to release some of its natural juices, 6 to 7 minutes.

4. Add the wine, if desired, and reduce it over high heat until nearly evaporated. Add the cream and simmer over low heat for about 5 minutes.

5. Meanwhile, bring about 1 inch of water to a rolling boil in a large skillet over high heat. Add the salt and the asparagus. Cover and pan-steam the asparagus until it is just tender and a deep green, 3 to 5 minutes.

6. Adjust the seasoning of the morel mixture with salt and pepper.

7. Drain the asparagus, place it on a heated serving platter or individual plates, and top with the morel-cream mixture. Scatter the toasted pistachios over the asparagus and serve at once.

Preceding Page:
Blue Cheese
Polenta

NUTRITION INFORMATION, PER SERVING (5 SPEARS): 198 calories, 5 grams protein, 17 grams fat, 9 grams carbohydrates, 290 milligrams sodium, 45 milligrams cholesterol.

AHEAD OF TIME: The leek and mushroom mixture may be prepared through step 3, and held in the refrigerator for up to 5 hours. Bring the mixture to room temperature before you steam the asparagus, then reheat gently.

PREPARATION NOTE: Peeling the asparagus is a little time-consuming, but it pays off in two ways. For one, the asparagus will be more tender and easier to eat. For another, the stems will cook as quickly as the tips, avoiding an age-old problem—soggy tips that fall away from crunchy stems.

VARIATIONS: Green beans can be substituted for the asparagus.

Morels are excellent for this, but when they are not available, shiitakes, portobellos, cremini, or cultivated white mushrooms also are excellent.

SERVING SUGGESTIONS: Serve this dish as a first course before salmon or halibut; or as an accompaniment for a simply grilled lamb chop or chicken breast.

Or, turn it into a main course for two by serving it over fresh linguine or fettuccine. For this, cut the asparagus on the bias into 2- to 3-inch pieces.

POTATO CHEDDAR CASSEROLE

*T*his popular potato dish, similar to *pommes Dauphinoise*, uses a technique known as *gratiner* which means it is baked until a golden brown crust forms.

MAKES 6 SERVINGS

4	russet potatoes	1	cup light cream or milk
1	tablespoon butter		Salt and freshly ground black pepper
1	tablespoon minced garlic		to taste
2	eggs	1	cup grated sharp Cheddar cheese

1. Preheat the oven to 300 degrees F. Peel the potatoes and hold them in a bowl of cool water.

2. Heat the butter in a small sauté pan over medium heat. Add the garlic and sauté just until soft, about 2 minutes; set aside.

3. Mix the eggs and cream together thoroughly, and season with salt and pepper. Add the garlic to the cream mixture.

4. Lightly grease a 9 x 11-inch baking pan or gratin dish. Slice the potatoes ¼ inch thick and arrange them in a single layer in the pan. Cover with one-quarter of the cream mixture and sprinkle with ¼ cup of the cheese. Continue layering until all the ingredients are used up, ending with cheese on the top.

5. Cover the pan loosely with foil and bake in the preheated oven for 45 to 50 minutes, until the potatoes are tender. Remove the foil and increase the oven temperature to 425 degrees F. Bake until the potatoes are brown on top.

NUTRITION INFORMATION, PER SERVING (½ CUP): 276 calories, 9 grams protein, 18 grams fat, 20 grams carbohydrates, 340 milligrams sodium, 140 milligrams cholesterol.

PREPARATION NOTES: For a silky texture, bake in a water bath at 275 degrees F for 80 to 90 minutes.

VARIATIONS: To give this casserole main-course status, add slivered ham; cooked green beans, peas, or asparagus; or sautéed onions or leeks.

SERVING SUGGESTIONS: Serve with baked ham, sautéed pork chops, or pot roast.

Winter Squashes with Dried Cranberries and Toasted Pecans

Squashes and cranberries have a natural affinity for one another. The tartness of these American berries gives a real boost to the subtle taste of squashes.

Makes 6 to 8 servings

1 cup vegetable (page 192) or chicken broth (page 193)

1 cup diced or julienned butternut squash

1 cup diced or julienned acorn squash

1 cup diced or julienned pumpkin

1 tablespoon dried cranberries, plumped (page 191)

¼ cup chopped toasted pecans (page 192)

2 tablespoons butter

Juice of 1 lemon

¼ teaspoon salt

⅛ teaspoon freshly ground black pepper

1. Bring the broth to a boil in a skillet over high heat. Add the squashes and pumpkin; cover the skillet and simmer over low heat just until tender, 10 to 12 minutes.

2. Remove the cover from the skillet, increase the heat to high, and allow any excess moisture to cook away, 2 to 3 minutes.

3. Drain the cranberries and add them to the skillet along with the nuts, butter, lemon juice, salt, and pepper. Continue to cook for another 2 minutes, stirring gently to distribute the ingredients evenly. Serve at once.

NUTRITION INFORMATION, PER SERVING (½ CUP): 105 calories, 3 grams protein, 6 grams fat, 135 grams carbohydrates, 320 milligrams sodium, 2 milligrams cholesterol.

PREPARATION NOTE: Whether diced or julienned, the squashes should all be the same size.

WILD RICE PATTIES

*W*ild rice has gone by many names. The Indians of the northern United States called it manomin. The French settlers of the late 1700s called it crazy oats. Other names, including Indian, Canadian, or Tuscarora rice, have been lost over time.

MAKES 6 SERVINGS

1 cup cooked wild rice	2 teaspoons chopped fresh parsley
1¼ cups mashed potatoes	½ teaspoon chopped fresh sage, or ¼
1 egg yolk	teaspoon dry
3 tablespoons sour cream	1 tablespoon fresh white bread crumbs
2 strips bacon, minced	¼ teaspoon salt
2 tablespoons minced scallions	⅛ teaspoon freshly ground black pepper
	Vegetable oil for frying

1. Combine cooked rice, mashed potatoes, egg yolk, and sour cream in a large bowl; set aside.
2. Sauté the bacon in a skillet over medium-high heat. Remove the bacon bits with a slotted spoon and drain on a paper towel.
3. Add the scallions, parsley, and sage to the bacon fat, and sauté for 2 to 4 minutes, or until the scallions are tender. Drain briefly to remove any excess fat.
4. Add the scallion mixture, crumbled bacon, and bread crumbs to the potato-rice mixture. Season with salt and pepper; cover the mixture and refrigerate for 10 to 15 minutes.
5. Heat about ⅓ inch of vegetable oil in a skillet. Shape the potato-rice mixture into 6 patties. Fry the patties over medium heat for 2 to 4 minutes per side, or until golden brown. Serve immediately.

NUTRITION INFORMATION, PER 3-INCH PATTY: 157 calories, 3 grams protein, 11 grams fat, 12 grams carbohydrates, 210 milligrams sodium, 55 milligrams cholesterol.

PREPARATION NOTE: To cook the wild rice, bring 1 cup of salted water to a boil. Add ½ cup rice and simmer for 35 to 40 minutes, or until tender.

SERVING SUGGESTIONS: This is a lovely first course for a game dinner.

Fresh Peas Stewed
in Minted Cream

*P*eas and mint have a natural affinity, and are welcome spring harbingers of the delights to come from gardens and farmer's markets. An old-fashioned touch is to add a few pods to give the peas a special sweetness as they steam.

Makes 4 servings

2	pounds peas in the pod	¼	cup light cream
2 to 3	cups water, or as needed	2	teaspoons chopped fresh mint
	Salt to taste	1 to 2	tablespoons butter (optional)
4	Boston lettuce leaves		

1. Shell the peas. Bring about 2 inches of water to a boil in a saucepan, and add salt to taste.
2. Add the peas and cover the pan. Pan-steam the peas for 3 to 4 minutes, or until they are brilliant green and quite tender. Drain the peas.
3. While the peas are steaming, shred the lettuce leaves and place them in a sauté pan along with the cream and mint over medium heat.
4. Transfer the cooked peas to the sauté pan. Simmer the peas and the lettuce-cream mixture for 2 to 3 minutes, or until the cream has thickened a bit.
5. Stir in the butter and season with salt to taste. Serve at once.

Nutrition information, per serving (½ cup): 150 calories, 8 grams protein, 6 grams fat, 17 grams carbohydrates, 149 milligrams sodium, 18 milligrams cholesterol.

Variation: Cooked pearl onions can be added to the peas as they stew in the cream and lettuce mixture.

Lower-fat Version: Substitute evaporated skimmed milk for the cream and omit the butter.

GARLIC-ROSEMARY POTATOES

*P*otatoes were first cultivated in the Andes mountains throughout South America. Since then literally thousands of distinct potato varieties have evolved. Exotic varieties with golden or purple skin and flesh are still grown today, though they are less widely available than the typical russet, all-purpose, and red bliss. If you can find Yukon or Finnish gold, purple, or black potatoes, use them for this recipe.

MAKES 4 SERVINGS

8 to 12	baby or new red potatoes (about ¾ pound)	1	garlic clove, minced
2	tablespoons butter	2	teaspoons chopped fresh rosemary leaves, plus additional sprigs for garnish
2	teaspoons freshly squeezed lemon juice		

1. Preheat the oven to 400 degrees F.

2. Rinse the potatoes and halve or cut them into wedges. Place them in a pot or deep sauté pan and add enough cold water to cover by 1 inch. Bring to a bare simmer over medium heat and cook for 10 minutes, or until the tip of a paring knife can be easily inserted through the first ¼ inch.

3. Pour off the water and return the pot to low heat; allow the potatoes to steam dry for 2 to 3 minutes.

4. Add the butter, lemon juice, garlic, and rosemary and toss or stir gently over medium heat until the garlic releases a rich aroma and the potatoes are evenly coated with butter.

5. Place the potatoes in a shallow baking dish and roast in the preheated oven, turning occasionally, until the skins are golden and the potatoes can be pierced easily with a fork, about 30 minutes. Garnish with the rosemary sprigs.

NUTRITION INFORMATION, PER SERVING (½ CUP): 193 calories, 3 grams protein, 7 grams fat, 32 grams carbohydrates, 68 milligrams sodium, 17 milligrams cholesterol.

SERVING SUGGESTIONS: These potatoes would make a good accompaniment for lamb or a nice change from the classic hash browns at brunch.

Garlic Cheese Grits Casserole

Grits and polenta share many similarities, but there is at least one major difference: Grits are usually made from white cornmeal while polenta is made from yellow.

Makes 8 servings

1 cup grits, long cooking, stone ground preferred	Tabasco or similar hot pepper sauce, to taste
1 teaspoon salt	½ teaspoon Worcestershire sauce
2 eggs, lightly beaten	Cayenne pepper to taste
1 clove garlic, minced	2 cups grated sharp Cheddar cheese
¾ cup milk	Salt to taste
	Freshly ground black pepper to taste

1. Bring 4 cups of water to a boil in a large pot. Preheat the oven to 350 degrees F.

2. Butter a shallow baking dish.

3. Stir grits and 1 teaspoon salt into the boiling water. Reduce the heat and simmer, stirring constantly, about 30 minutes or until thick. Remove from the heat.

4. Mix together the eggs, garlic, milk, Tabasco, Worcestershire, and cayenne. Add mixture and 1½ cups of the cheese to the grits. Add salt and pepper to taste.

5. Pour mixture into the buttered dish.

6. Bake in the preheated oven until firm, about 20 minutes. Top with the remaining grated cheese and bake an additional 10 minutes.

Nutrition information, per serving (½ cup): 220 calories, 11 grams protein, 12 grams fat, 18 grams carbohydrates, 340 milligrams sodium, 100 milligrams cholesterol.

Preparation Note: For a more elegant touch, this recipe can easily be turned into a soufflé by separating the 2 eggs, adding the yolks with the milk and seasonings, and then folding in 3 beaten egg whites. Bake in a preheated 375-degree F oven for 45 minutes.

Variations: Fresh, seeded, chopped jalapeños or other green chiles can be added; smoked cheese can be used in place of the Cheddar.

BAKED BEANS

*B*aked beans were a Sunday staple in early Puritan settlements because of the prohibition against cooking on the Sabbath. This dish, along with Boston Brown Bread (page 143), can be prepared on Saturday and set to bake overnight.

MAKES 12 SERVINGS

2 cups dried navy or Great Northern beans, soaked overnight (page 191)	¼ cup molasses
8 slices bacon, diced	1 teaspoon dry mustard
1 onion, diced	Salt to taste
½ cup brown sugar	Freshly ground black pepper to taste

1. Drain the beans and place them in a pot with enough fresh, cool water to cover. Bring to a boil over medium-high heat; reduce heat and simmer for 2 hours, or until a bean is tender enough to mash easily.

2. Preheat the oven to 350 degrees F. Drain excess water from the beans and place them in an ovenproof casserole.

3. Cook the bacon over medium-high heat in a heavy skillet until limp. Using a slotted spoon, transfer the bacon to paper towels to drain. Add the bacon to the beans.

4. Add the onions to the rendered bacon fat and cook over medium-low heat until tender and slightly brown. Add the onion to the beans.

5. Add the brown sugar, molasses, and mustard to the beans and stir to blend thoroughly.

6. Season with salt and pepper.

7. Cover the casserole loosely with foil and bake in the preheated oven 3 to 4 hours. If the beans seem too dry, add up to ½ cup water. The beans are done when the liquid is very thick.

NUTRITION INFORMATION, PER SERVING (½ CUP): 200 calories, 8 grams protein, 5 grams fat, 33 grams carbohydrates, 125 milligrams sodium, 5 milligrams cholesterol.

SERVING SUGGESTIONS: This is a classic accompaniment for hot dogs, hamburgers, or meatloaf. It is a perfect dish to take to a potluck dinner, because it is only worth the bother when you make a big batch.

Red Beans and Rice

Red beans and rice are a Monday tradition in New Orleans. There is no small amount of debate over certain particulars: whether kidney beans are better than a smaller version found in Southern Louisiana; whether the beans and rice should be cooked together or separately; or whether sweet pickled pork is essential.

MAKES 6 SERVINGS

¾ cup red beans, soaked overnight (page 191)

¼ pound smoked ham

¼ pound Andouille or other smoked sausage, cut into 1-inch cubes (optional)

1 yellow onion, diced

2 stalks celery, diced

1 green pepper, diced

¼ cup chopped fresh parsley

1 bay leaf

1 teaspoon chopped fresh thyme leaves

3 garlic cloves, crushed

1 tablespoon Worcestershire sauce, or to taste

Tabasco or similar hot pepper sauce to taste

½ teaspoon salt, or to taste

¼ teaspoon freshly ground black pepper, or to taste

2 cups cooked rice

1. Drain the beans and combine them in a soup pot with enough fresh, cold water to cover by 2 inches. Bring the water to a rolling boil over high heat. Reduce the heat to medium, and simmer the beans until they are tender to the bite, about 1½ hours; do not overcook. Add water as needed to keep the beans covered during cooking.

2. Add the remaining ingredients, except the rice, and water as needed to keep the beans barely covered. Simmer for another 45 minutes to 1 hour, or until the liquid has thickened.

3. Adjust the seasonings and serve over the cooked rice.

NUTRITION INFORMATION, PER SERVING (½ CUP): 215 calories, 10 grams protein, 8 grams fat, 25 grams carbohydrates, 460 milligrams sodium, 20 milligrams cholesterol.

SERVING SUGGESTIONS: Serve as a side dish or as a satisfying main dish with cooked greens or a big salad.

BRAISED BLACK BEANS

*C*horizo is a traditional spicy Mexican sausage used extensively as a flavoring agent. It is an exceptional match for any bean-based dish. A dollop of sour cream, yogurt, or salsa is a refreshing garnish for this flavorful side dish.

MAKES 6 TO 8 SERVINGS

1	pound black beans, soaked overnight (page 191)	½	red pepper, diced
4	ounces chorizo, removed from casing and crumbled	½	jalapeño pepper or to taste, minced
1	tablespoon vegetable oil	¼	cup red wine
2 to 3	garlic cloves, minced	1	tablespoon cider vinegar
1	onion, diced	½	cup water
			Salt to taste
			Freshly ground black pepper to taste

1. Drain the beans and place them in a pot with enough fresh, cool water to cover by 2 inches. Simmer over medium heat for 45 minutes, or until a bean is tender enough to mash easily.
2. Sauté the chorizo in a skillet over low heat until fat is rendered, 3 to 4 minutes. With a slotted spoon transfer the meat to paper towels to drain; set aside.
3. Heat the oil in a pot over medium heat. Add the garlic, onion, red pepper, and jalapeño, and sauté for 6 to 8 minutes.
4. Add the red wine and scrape up any brown bits from the bottom of the pot. Add the drained beans, vinegar, and water.
5. Add the drained chorizo to the beans, cover, and braise over low heat for 30 to 40 minutes.
6. Taste and season with salt and pepper.

NUTRITION INFORMATION, PER SERVING (½ CUP): 270 calories, 17 grams protein, 6 grams fat, 40 grams carbohydrates, 270 milligrams sodium, 10 milligrams cholesterol.

VARIATIONS: Italian or hot fresh or cured sausage may be substituted for chorizo. Cumin and chili powder can be added if a spicier flavor is desired.

SERVING SUGGESTIONS: These beans can be a main-course served over steamed rice. Top with diced red onions and strips of toasted corn tortillas.

BRAISED FENNEL

*B*raising is an excellent method for many vegetables, including celery, romaine lettuce, carrots, parsnips, Belgian endive, or red cabbage. Fennel, sometimes called anise because of its distinct licorice flavor, is found in late fall and early winter.

MAKES 4 SERVINGS

1 cup chicken (page 193) or vegetable broth (page 192)

2 fennel bulbs, trimmed and cut length-wise into eighths

2 plum tomatoes, peeled, seeded, and chopped (page 191)

1 tablespoon chopped fresh parsley

1 tablespoon freshly squeezed lemon juice

¼ teaspoon salt

⅛ teaspoon freshly ground black pepper

1. Preheat the oven to 350 degrees F. Bring the broth to a boil.

2. Place the pieces of fennel in a baking dish and add the broth. Cover tightly with aluminum foil and bake in the preheated oven until the fennel can be easily pierced with a paring knife, about 45 minutes.

3. Add the chopped tomatoes, parsley, lemon juice, salt, and pepper to the baking dish; replace the cover and cook for 10 more minutes.

4. Spoon a bit of the broth and tomatoes over each serving.

NUTRITION INFORMATION, PER SERVING (½ CUP): 36 calories, 2 grams protein, 1 gram fat, 7 grams carbohydrates, 230 milligrams sodium, 82 milligrams cholesterol.

VARIATIONS: Replace fennel with celery hearts or Belgian endive. To prepare celery hearts, trim away the root end and cut in half lengthwise. Use the tip of a paring knife to cut away the core of the endive. It also is a good idea to quickly blanch endive for 2 to 3 minutes in boiling salted water before braising.

SERVING SUGGESTIONS: This is a nice side dish with roasted chicken or turkey. It also is a good addition to the traditional Thanksgiving feast.

CREOLE VEGETABLES

*V*egetable stews such as this one play a large role in Acadian cookery. Unlike some more contemporary vegetable dishes, long gentle cooking is required to achieve the rich, velvety texture and multilayered flavors expected in this dish.

MAKES 6 SERVINGS

3 slices bacon	4 plum tomatoes, peeled, seeded, and chopped (page 191)
1 onion, chopped	
3 cloves garlic, minced	3 scallions, trimmed and chopped
1 cup quartered mushrooms	¼ teaspoon ground cumin
1 red pepper, seeded and chopped	1 teaspoon fresh oregano
1 green pepper, seeded and chopped	2 tablespoons chopped fresh parsley
1 stalk celery, chopped	Tabasco sauce, to taste
1 zucchini, diced	Salt to taste
2 cups okra, trimmed and blanched	Freshly ground black pepper to taste
½ cup red or black beans, soaked overnight in water (page 191)	

1. Cook the bacon in a skillet over medium-high heat until crisp. Remove with a slotted spoon and drain on paper towels.

2. Pour off most of the fat from the skillet. Add the onions and cook over medium heat until translucent, about 5 minutes.

3. Add the garlic and mushrooms, and sauté 2 to 3 minutes. Add the peppers and celery, and sauté another 2 to 3 minutes.

4. Add the zucchini and cook until almost tender, about 5 minutes.

5. Add the okra, beans, tomatoes, scallions, cumin, and oregano, and stir to combine.

6. Add enough water to cover beans by 1 inch and simmer for 45 minutes, or until beans are fork tender, adding more water if necessary.

7. Adjust the seasonings and add the parsley and Tabasco. Remove from the heat and let stand for 10 to 12 minutes.

NUTRITION INFORMATION, PER SERVING (½ CUP): 110 calories, 5 grams protein, 4 grams fat, 16 grams carbohydrates, 262 milligrams sodium, 6 milligrams cholesterol.

PREPARATION NOTES: Select okra pods that are an appealing color, with no withered or soft spots. The smaller the pod, the shorter the overall cooking time will be.

Use precooked or drained and rinsed canned beans to shorten the cooking time.

SERVING SUGGESTIONS: This dish is paired with Braised Lamb Shanks (page 100) but would also be good on its own as an entrée. Serve it with plenty of steamed rice, corn bread, and a big salad. Follow with Pecan Pie (page 177) and a pot of steaming coffee.

Kale with
Hot Bacon Vinaigrette

*M*ost people have only experienced kale as an overcooked, tangled, pea-green pulp. This recipe, which yields flavorful and tender greens that retain their attractive bright green color, can turn kale bashers into kale lovers.

MAKES 4 SERVINGS

1	pound kale, carefully washed and tough stems removed	1	tablespoon olive oil
4	slices raw bacon, chopped	½	teaspoon salt, or to taste
1	tablespoon minced shallots	¼	teaspoon freshly ground black pepper, or to taste
2	tablespoons champagne vinegar		

1. Place about 1 inch of water in a large skillet and bring it to a boil. Add the kale, cover the skillet, and cook over high heat for about 5 minutes or until the kale is wilted, but still bright green. Drain the kale in a colander and rinse with cool water.

2. Sauté the bacon in the skillet over medium-high heat until brown and crisp. Remove the bacon with a slotted spoon and drain on paper towels.

3. Add the shallots to the bacon fat and cook for another 2 minutes, stirring constantly. Add the vinegar and oil. Whisk the vinaigrette well.

4. Add the drained kale to the skillet and toss it to coat evenly with the vinaigrette.

5. Season the kale to taste with salt and pepper. Scatter the bacon over the kale.

NUTRITION INFORMATION, PER SERVING (½ CUP): 120 calories, 7 grams protein, 8 grams fat, 8 grams carbohydrates, 391 milligrams sodium, 4 milligrams cholesterol.

VARIATION: For a meatless version of this dish, sauté the shallots and blanched kale in 3 tablespoons of good-quality olive oil.

SERVING SUGGESTION: This side dish goes well with Red Beans and Rice (page 111).

BUTTERMILK MASHED POTATOES

*O*ne of the all-time favorite comfort foods, whipped potatoes can be sublime when care is applied to the entire process. All-purpose, or chef's, potatoes have the creamiest texture. Don't skip the drying step—it really helps to develop a robust potato flavor. Heating the buttermilk and butter produces a light, silky dish. Whipped potatoes are best eaten as soon as possible after they are prepared.

MAKES 4 SERVINGS

2 to 3	all-purpose potatoes, peeled and cut into 2-inch cubes		2	tablespoons snipped fresh chives
3	tablespoons (or more) unsalted butter		½	teaspoon salt, or to taste
⅓	cup (or more) buttermilk		¼	teaspoon freshly ground black pepper, or to taste

1. Place the potatoes in a pot and add enough cold water to cover. Bring to a simmer over medium heat and cook until the potatoes can be easily pierced with a paring knife, 25 to 30 minutes.

2. Drain the potatoes and return them to the pot. Cover and let them steam dry over low heat for 3 to 4 minutes.

3. Meanwhile, heat the butter and buttermilk in a stainless steel saucepan over low heat until the butter has melted and the milk is hot.

4. Purée the potatoes into a large bowl through a strainer, food mill, or potato ricer while still very hot.

5. Whip in the heated buttermilk and butter, adding more if necessary to achieve a light, fluffy texture.

6. Add chives and salt and pepper to taste, and serve at once.

NUTRITION INFORMATION, PER SERVING (½ CUP): 126 calories, 3 grams protein, 7 grams fat, 17 grams carbohydrates, 280 milligrams sodium, 17 milligrams cholesterol.

PREPARATION NOTES: If you use a food mill, you can eliminate peeling the potatoes. It is important that the potatoes be very hot when they are puréed. Do not use a blender or food processor, however, or the potatoes will become too runny.

Corn Pancakes

*T*his pancake batter incorporates puréed corn as well as whole corn kernels for a wonderful layering of flavors and textures. Pass a platter of these tender cakes topped with Guacamole (page 127) for a special hors d'oeuvre.

MAKES 8 TO 10 PANCAKES (ABOUT 4 INCHES IN DIAMETER)

1½	cups fresh or frozen corn kernels, blanched	½	jalapeño, minced, or to taste
2	tablespoons butter	1	tablespoon minced fresh basil leaves
3	scallions, chopped	¾	cup all-purpose flour
3	tablespoons dry white wine (optional)	⅓	cup yellow cornmeal
½	cup half-and-half	½	teaspoon baking powder
3	eggs	½	teaspoon salt
1	tablespoon honey	½	teaspoon freshly ground black pepper

1. Purée 1 cup of the corn kernels in a food processor.

2. Heat the butter in a skillet over high heat. Add the scallions and sauté until they are tender, 2 to 3 minutes.

3. Add the wine to the skillet and continue to cook until most of it has cooked away, about 3 minutes. Transfer the scallions to a medium bowl and allow them to cool slightly.

4. Add the half-and-half, eggs, the puréed and whole corn kernels, honey, jalapeño, and basil to the scallions; mix well.

5. Combine the flour, cornmeal, baking powder, salt, and pepper in a separate bowl and stir to blend. Add the wet ingredients and stir until a relatively smooth batter forms. Do not overbeat.

6. Preheat a griddle or cast-iron skillet over medium-high heat; oil lightly. For each pancake, ladle about ¼ cup of batter onto the griddle. Cook the pancakes on the first side until the edges begin to look set. Flip the pancake, and finish cooking on the second side until golden brown, another 2 minutes. Remove and serve at once.

NUTRITION INFORMATION, PER PANCAKE: 180 calories, 6 grams protein, 7 grams fat, 24 grams carbohydrates, 190 milligrams sodium, 120 milligrams cholesterol.

PREPARATION NOTES: This recipe doubles readily. You can keep the pancakes warm as you prepare them, in a baking dish, loosely covered with waxed or parchment paper, in a 200-degree F oven.

AHEAD OF TIME: Stack the cooked and cooled pancakes with a square of waxed paper separating each. Wrap and freeze the stacks for up to 6 weeks. To reheat, warm frozen pancakes in a 250-degree F oven for 12 to 15 minutes, or for 8 to 10 minutes if thawed.

VARIATION: Substitute ¾ cup puréed black or pinto beans for ¾ cup of the corn.

SERVING SUGGESTIONS: Made small, these pancakes would be nice with salsa, sour cream, and grated cheese, as an appetizer. They would also make an excellent accompaniment for grilled meat and vegetables and Braised Black Beans (page 112).

BLUE CHEESE POLENTA

*T*his variation on traditional cornmeal squares calls for American Maytag blue cheese rather than Italian Gorgonzola.

MAKES 12 SERVINGS

6	cups cold water	2	tablespoons chopped fresh thyme
1½	cups yellow cornmeal, stone ground, if available	1	cup Maytag blue cheese, crumbled
½	teaspoon freshly grated nutmeg	½	stick unsalted butter
2	tablespoons chopped fresh rosemary	1	teaspoon salt
		½	teaspoon freshly ground black pepper

1. Grease a 9 x 13-inch baking dish well and set aside.

2. Pour the cold water into a large saucepan and bring to a simmer over medium heat. Add the polenta very gradually, stirring constantly.

3. Continue to stir until the polenta pulls away from the sides of the pot, about 40 minutes.

4. As soon as the polenta is fully cooked, add the nutmeg, rosemary, thyme, blue cheese, butter, salt, and pepper, and stir to combine.

5. Pour the mixture onto the prepared sheet and cover tightly with plastic wrap; there should be no ridges on the surface.

6. Chill the polenta in the refregerator for 2 to 3 hours, or overnight, until it is firm. Cut into shapes—squares, diamonds, or circles—and place them on a second baking sheet, leaving room between. Preheat the oven to 375 degrees F and bake for 20 minutes.

7. Brown the polenta under the broiler until golden on top, 2 to 3 minutes. Serve immediately.

NUTRITION INFORMATION, PER SERVING (1 CUP): 153 calories, 4 grams protein, 12 grams fat, 8 grams carbohydrates, 730 milligrams sodium, 30 milligrams cholesterol.

SERVING SUGGESTIONS: Add 1 cup cooked, crumbled bacon or finely diced, sautéed green or red bell peppers with the other ingredients and serve the squares as appetizers. Or, serve as a side dish or as the main course for a simple supper.

Condiments

HOME-STYLE HERBED CHEESE

*T*his delicious fresh cheese takes very little time to prepare, and it can be almost endlessly varied to suit your taste, your budget, and the season.

MAKES 1½ CUPS (ABOUT 10 SERVINGS)

1 8-ounce package cream cheese	1 teaspoon chopped fresh thyme
3 tablespoons unsalted butter	2 teaspoons chopped fresh chives
2 tablespoons mayonnaise	1 teaspoon chopped fresh dill
2 teaspoons Dijon mustard	½ teaspoon chopped fresh rosemary
2 to 3 garlic cloves, finely minced	Pinch of cayenne pepper
2 tablespoons freshly grated Parmesan cheese	½ teaspoon salt
	¼ teaspoon freshly ground black pepper

1. Allow the cream cheese and butter to come to room temperature, or soften them in the microwave oven at the lowest power setting.

2. Combine all the ingredients in a bowl and blend well with a wooden spoon.

3. Cover the cheese and store it in the refrigerator for at least 24 hours.

NUTRITION INFORMATION, PER SERVING (ABOUT 2½ TABLESPOONS): 125 calories, 2 grams protein, 12 grams fat, 2 grams carbohydrates, 200 milligrams sodium, 35 milligrams cholesterol.

LOWER-FAT VERSION: To reduce the fat and calories in this cheese, substitute drained low- or nonfat yogurt for part of the cheese: Set the yogurt in a colander lined with cheesecloth or a clean linen towel for at least 12 hours. Blend with about ¼ cup of softened cream cheese. Replace the butter and mayonnaise with low-fat or regular sour cream. In this version, the cheese will have a slightly more tart, less rich flavor.

VARIATIONS: Any fresh herbs or fresh parsley combined with dried fresh herbs can be used. Sautéed (and cooled) onions, garlic, leeks, or shallots; finely chopped fresh or roasted bell peppers or hot chiles (page 191); grated aged goat cheese or blue cheese can be added.

SERVING SUGGESTIONS: Serve this cheese as a spread with whole-wheat walnut bread, pumpernickel raisin, or other hearty whole-grain loaves. It also makes a fine dip for crudité.

*Preceding Page:
Home-style
Herbed Cheese
with Flatbread*

Salsa is the Spanish word for "sauce." With the growing popularity of Southwestern, Tex-Mex, and Mexican foods throughout the country, it has taken on a particular meaning—we think of it as a fresh raw sauce made with tomatoes, chiles, peppers, and onions, and seasoned with vinegar, lemon or lime juice, and fresh herbs. The possible variations on the salsa theme make it one of the most versatile sauces in contemporary American cooking.

MAKES 2 CUPS

4 plum tomatoes (about 1 pound), seeded and chopped (page 191)	2 tablespoons red wine vinegar
1 jalapeño pepper, roasted, peeled, and minced (page 191)	½ teaspoon salt, or to taste
1 red onion, minced	¼ teaspoon freshly ground black pepper, or to taste

1. Mix together the tomatoes, jalapeño, onion, and vinegar in a bowl. Add salt and pepper to taste.

2. Refrigerate, covered, for at least 2 hours before serving.

NUTRITION INFORMATION, PER SERVING (ABOUT ¼ CUP): 20 calories, 1 gram protein, trace of fat, 5 milligrams carbohydrates, 135 milligrams sodium, 0 milligrams cholesterol.

VARIATIONS: Fresh herbs, such as oregano, parsely, chives, or cilantro, can be added. To make a relatively smooth sauce, purée the salsa in a food processor or blender to the desired consistency.

Tomatillos, a relative of the gooseberry, can be substituted for all or some of the tomatoes. To prepare tomatillos, peel away the papery husk and rinse. Cut large tomatillos into halves or quarters. Blanch tomatillos briefly, about 2 to 3 minutes, in enough rapidly boiling water to cover. Drain them, rinse with cool water, and chop finely.

SERVING SUGGESTIONS: Salsa is typically accompanied by a basket of tortilla chips to start a meal. It can also be served as the sauce for grilled tuna or swordfish steaks; as a topping for tacos, nachos, or enchiladas; or as a zesty addition to a bowl of simmered beans served over rice.

Roasted Corn Salsa

oasted corn is a universal treat. In Mexico, India, and South East Asia, it is roasted on the street, and seasoned with chiles, salt, and lime juice. In North America corn was traditionally roasted in ash by Native Americans.

Corn roasted over charcoal develops a wonderful flavor. Dampen the corn husks and place them over glowing coals. Grill, turning occasionally to ensure even roasting, until the kernels are tender and a light golden brown, about 15 minutes. This salsa combines the sweet, smoky corn with roasted pepper.

Makes 2 cups

2	ears of fresh corn, husks on	1	teaspoon chopped fresh oregano
1	red pepper, halved and seeded	½	teaspoon kosher salt, or to taste
¼	cup extra-virgin olive oil	¼	teaspoon freshly ground black pepper,
¼	cup freshly squeezed lime juice		or to taste
2	teaspoons chopped fresh parsley		

1. Preheat the oven to 475 degrees F. Dampen the corn husks well, and place the corn on a baking sheet. Place the pepper, cut side down, on the baking sheet. Roast until the corn is tender and the pepper is blackened, about 20 minutes. Place the pepper in a bowl and cover tightly; set aside for 10 minutes. Set the corn aside until it is cool enough to handle.

2. Pull the husks and silk from the corn and cut the kernels from the cob into a bowl. Peel the skin from the pepper, and cut it into a neat dice. Add the pepper to the corn.

3. Combine the olive oil, lime juice, parsley, oregano, salt, and pepper in a small bowl and mix well. Add this vinaigrette to the corn and peppers. Set aside at room temperature for at least 30 minutes, or cover tightly and store in the refrigerator for up to 4 days.

NUTRITION INFORMATION, PER SERVING (¼ TO ⅓ CUP): 120 calories, 1 gram protein, 9 grams fat, 9 grams carbohydrates, 175 milligrams sodium, 0 milligrams cholesterol.

VARIATION: This salsa can be made as hot as you like, by adding some chopped hot peppers or chiles when you combine the other ingredients. Be aware that acids, like lime juice, bring out the heat of chiles, and remember that you can always add a little more just before serving.

SERVING SUGGESTION: Serve with grilled quesadillas or empanadas.

Chayote Jícama Salsa

*T*his quickly prepared salsa incorporates two ingredients well-known in South America and Mexico and, in this country, in California and the Southwest. It is more recently that jícama and chayote have made a noticeable appearance throughout the United States.

MAKES 2 TO 3 CUPS

1 chayote squash (about ¼ pound), peeled and diced	½ cup diced red onion
1 jícama (about ¼ to ½ pound), peeled and diced	1 tablespoon (or more) cider vinegar
2 tomatoes, peeled, seeded, and diced (page 191)	½ teaspoon salt, or to taste
1 jalapeño, finely minced	¼ teaspoon freshly ground black pepper, or to taste
	Tabasco or similar hot pepper sauce to taste

1. Bring about 1 inch of water to a rolling boil over high heat in a sauté pan. Add the diced chayote and cover the pan; steam the squash for about 4 minutes, or until it is just barely translucent (it should offer slight resistance when pierced with a fork); do not let the squash become mushy. Drain and rinse the chayote under cool water to stop the cooking.

2. Combine the chayote with the remaining ingredients in a bowl.

3. Chill the salsa for 2 to 3 hours or overnight.

4. Taste the salsa and adjust the seasonings with additional vinegar, salt, pepper, or hot sauce.

NUTRITION INFORMATION, PER SERVING (¼ TO ⅓ CUP): 24 calories, 1 gram protein, less than 1 gram fat, 6 grams carbohydrates, 175 milligrams sodium, 0 milligrams cholesterol.

PREPARATION NOTES: To peel chayote, use a vegetable peeler. For jícama use a sharp paring knife: Halve or quarter legthwise, then pull and slice away the skin and the fibrous layer just below.

VARIATIONS: Add diced mango, papaya, oranges, or pineapple instead of tomatoes; julienned red peppers and green onions cut on the bias will turn this into a full-fledged salad.

SERVING SUGGESTIONS: Serve as a side dish with fajitas, enchiladas, or burritos; on its own as a first course; or with freshly toasted corn tortillas with margaritas or other cocktails.

Smoked Jalapeño Salsa

Smoked jalapeños, also known as *chipotles,* can be purchased in specialty grocery stores that carry Latin American foods. They are canned in a fiery hot sauce, known as *adobo,* which is included in this salsa for a little extra kick.

Makes 1½ cups

2	tomatoes, chopped	1	garlic clove, minced
½	cup tomato juice	2	tablespoons minced fresh cilantro
2	tablespoons canned chipotle peppers, chopped		Juice of 1 lime
1	teaspoon adobo sauce (optional)	¼	teaspoon salt, or to taste
¼	cup diced red onion	¼	teaspoon freshly ground black pepper, or to taste

Combine all the ingredients in a bowl and stir to combine evenly. Cover the bowl and store the salsa overnight in the refrigerator to allow the flavors to develop.

Nutrition information, per serving (about 3 tablespoons): 35 calories, 2 grams protein, trace of fat, 8 grams carbohydrates, 275 milligrams sodium, 0 milligrams cholesterol.

Variation: Fresh or canned jalapeños or other chiles can be substituted for the chipotles according to availability and taste.

Serving Suggestions: This salsa is a good choice for aficionados of hot, spicy foods. Serve it with grilled poultry, fish, or even vegetables. Have some sour cream, beer, or plain rice available to staunch the flames.

GUACAMOLE

*T*hough it is rarely thought of as such, guacamole is a raw sauce. The classic recipe calls for fresh, ripe avocados lightly seasoned with salt, pepper, lime juice, and fresh cilantro, but there are countless variations. Additional ingredients can alter the flavor, texture, and color. In any case, the keys to a successful guacamole are using ripe avocadoes, making the sauce as close to the time you plan to serve it as possible, and having a light hand with seasonings to allow the subtle taste and unctuous texture of the avocado to shine.

MAKES APPROXIMATELY 4 SERVINGS

1	avocado	1	tablespoon chopped fresh cilantro
	Finely grated zest and juice of one	⅛	teaspoon salt, or to taste
	lime, kept separate		Freshly ground black pepper to taste

1. Peel, pit, and dice the avocado. Mash the avocado and lime juice together to form a coarsely textured paste. Fold in the lime zest, cilantro, salt, and freshly ground pepper.

2. Serve at once. If necessary, guacamole may be stored in a bowl in the refrigerator for a few hours. To prevent discoloration, lay a piece of plastic wrap or waxed paper directly on the surface of the guacamole to make an air-tight seal.

NUTRITION INFORMATION, PER SERVING (¼ CUP): 80 calories, 5 grams protein, 37 grams fat, 15 milligrams carbohydrates, 280 milligrams sodium, 0 milligrams cholesterol.

PREPARATION NOTES: Avocados discolor quickly and should be prepared just before using. To halve and peel an avocado, make an incision from top to bottom and twist gently to separate the halves. Pull or cut away the skin, and gently pry out the pit.

VARIATIONS: Add chili powder or a few dashes of Tabasco or other hot pepper sauce.

Add chopped tomatoes, chopped peppers or chiles, corn kernels, diced red onion, and shredded jícama to make an avocado salad.

SERVING SUGGESTIONS: Guacamole can be served on its own as a dip, as a filling for tacos, as a cool accompaniment to spicy Southwestern dishes or blackened fish, or as an addition to sandwiches.

Overleaf:
Salsa and
Guacamole

DRIED CHERRY AND APPLE CHUTNEY

*C*hutneys are usually made from fruits or vegetables simmered together with spices, vinegar, and sugar to create a delicious sweet-sour condiment. This one uses a combination of fresh and dried fruits.

MAKES 1 TO 1½ CUPS

3 tablespoons vegetable oil	2 tablespoons sherry wine vinegar
½ cup minced onion	2 tablespoons water
1 Granny Smith apple, peeled, cored, and diced	½ teaspoon salt, or to taste
½ cup dried cherries	Cayenne pepper to taste
2 tablespoons sugar	Freshly grated nutmeg to taste
½ orange, peeled, chopped, and seeds removed	

1. Heat the oil in a sauté pan over high heat; add the onion and sauté until golden brown, 7 to 8 minutes.

2. Add the apple, cherries, sugar, orange, vinegar, and water; bring to a full boil.

3. Reduce the heat to low and simmer 7 to 8 minutes, or until the chutney thickens very slightly.

4. Remove the sauté pan from the heat. Add salt, cayenne, and nutmeg; cool to room temperature. Serve immediately or store in clean jars in the refrigerator for up to 2 weeks.

NUTRITION INFORMATION, PER SERVING (ABOUT **2** TABLESPOONS): 85 calories, less than 1 gram protein, 5 grams fat, 11 grams carbohydrates, 5 milligrams sodium, 0 milligrams cholesterol.

VARIATIONS: Dried pineapple, apricots, blueberries, or cranberries can be substituted for the cherries.

SERVING SUGGESTIONS: Serve with roasted or grilled chicken, duck, pork, or ham. It is also delicious spread over hearty whole-grain breads.

RED CURRY PASTE

*L*emon grass, spices, and chiles are combined to make this curry paste.

MAKES ABOUT 1 CUP

1	teaspoon coriander seeds	1	canned chipotle pepper
½	teaspoon fennel seeds	2	tablespoons olive oil
½	teaspoon cumin seeds	1	shallot, minced
½	teaspoon whole black peppercorns	3	garlic cloves, minced
1	stalk lemon grass	1	tablespoon gingerroot, minced
2	red bell peppers, roasted, peeled, and seeded (page 191)	¼	teaspoon freshly grated nutmeg Zest from 1 lime, grated
3	jalapeño peppers, seeded	½	teaspoon salt

1. Combine the coriander, fennel, cumin, and black pepper in a small baking dish and toast in the oven at 350 degrees F for 5 minutes. Remove and cool slightly. Grind in a spice or coffee grinder or mortar and pestle.

2. Cut away the bottom 4 inches of the lemon grass, peel away the tough outer layer, and mince or chop the inside stalk.

3. Combine the spices and lemon grass with the remaining ingredients in a blender or food processor and purée until the mixture is a fine paste. Store it in a clean jar or dish, cover tightly, and refrigerate; it will keep well for at least 3 weeks.

NUTRITION INFORMATION PER TABLESPOON: 42 calories, trace of protein, 2 grams fat, 2 grams carbohydrates, 100milligrams sodium, 0 milligrams cholesterol

PREPARATION NOTES: Besides the Steamed Maine Mussels with Spicy Red Curry (page 28), Red Curry Paste also can be used to flavor other dishes, such as stir-frys or stews of chicken, fish, or seafood.

HEYWOOD'S MUSTARD

Jim Heywood, of the CIA, is famous for his wonderful "pantry" foods—items that most people might not make from scratch. This mustard in particular has become a favorite.

MAKES APPROXIMATELY 1 CUP

⅓	cup dry mustard	⅔	cup malt vinegar
1	tablespoon sugar	1	teaspoon honey
¾	teaspoon salt	½	teaspoon Tabasco or similar hot
3	large eggs		pepper sauce

1. Bring about 2 inches of water to a boil in the bottom of a double boiler, and reduce the heat to low.

2. Whisk the mustard, sugar, salt, and eggs together in the top of the double boiler. Add the malt vinegar and mix well.

3. Whisk this mixture over the simmering water until the mustard has thickened. It should fall from the whisk in ribbons that remain visible on the surface for several seconds. Take care not to let the mixture boil or it will curdle.

4. Remove the mustard from the heat, and stir in the honey and hot pepper sauce. Cool to room temperature, then place in a clean bowl or jar, cover tightly, and chill thoroughly before serving. The mustard may be stored in the refrigerator for up to 2 weeks.

NUTRITION INFORMATION, PER SERVING (1 TABLESPOON): 35 calories, 2 grams protein, 2 grams fat, 3 grams carbohydrates, 110 milligrams sodium, 40 milligrams cholesterol.

VARIATIONS: Use this mustard as a base to create specialty mustards:

GREEN PEPPERCORN MUSTARD: Add 1 to 2 teaspoons of mashed green peppercorns. (Use a brine-packed variety.)

HERB MUSTARD: Add 1 to 2 tablespoons chopped fresh herbs. Use a single herb or a combination as desired. Good choices include dill, chives, tarragon, chervil, oregano, marjoram, and basil.

HORSERADISH MUSTARD: Add 1 tablespoon grated fresh or drained bottled horseradish, or to taste, and freshly cracked black pepper.

Allow these mustards to rest for several days to a week in the refrigerator.

RED ONION MARMALADE

Marmalades are similar to jams and jellies, but the ingredients are handled differently. Jellies are made from the juice of fruits and vegetables; jams from the whole food. Conserves and marmalades usually leave the food whole, chunky, or thinly sliced. While orange marmalade may be the classic we all think of instantly, this quickly prepared version is a wonderful counterpoint to the quickly grilled and sautéed foods featured in many American meals today.

MAKES 1 CUP

2	medium red onions, thinly sliced	¼	teaspoon salt
2	tablespoons dry red wine	¼	teaspoon freshly ground black pepper
2	teaspoons sugar	1	teaspoon chopped fresh thyme, or ½
2	teaspoons Grenadine		teaspoon dried leaves
2	teaspoons cider vinegar		

1. Combine all the ingredients except the thyme in a saucepan; simmer over medium-low heat until most of the liquid has evaporated.

2. Remove the pan from the heat and add the thyme.

3. The marmalade may be served immediately, or cooled and stored. To store, transfer the room-temperature marmalade to a clean jar or bowl. Cover tightly and refrigerate. The marmalade will keep, refrigerated, for up to 10 days.

NUTRITION INFORMATION, PER SERVING (2 TABLESPOONS): 25 calories, less than 1 gram protein, trace of fat, 5 grams carbohydrates, 70 milligrams sodium, 0 milligrams cholesterol.

VARIATION: This marmalade could be made with Vidalia or other sweet onions. Use a white wine instead of red wine for the best appearance, or try a dry sherry or vermouth.

SERVING SUGGESTIONS: This marmalade is a delicious garnish for roasted meats, fish, and poultry. It is especially good with Grilled Duck Breast (page 78), grilled steaks, and pork chops. Also try it with Wild Mushroom-Potato Cakes (page 26) or Crab Cakes (page 12).

TOMATO-GINGER COULIS

MAKES 2 CUPS

¼	cup vegetable oil
¼	pound peeled and grated gingerroot
4	tomatoes, peeled, seeded, and chopped (page 191)
¼	teaspoon salt, or to taste
¼	teaspoon freshly ground black pepper, or to taste
1	tablespoon vinegar, or to taste

1. Heat the oil in a small saucepan over medium heat and add the ginger. Remove the pan from the heat and set aside to steep for at least 15 minutes. Remove and strain; discard the gingerroot.

2. Purée the tomato, salt, pepper, and vinegar in a blender. Add the infused oil and blend until emulsified.

NUTRITIONAL INFORMATION, PER SERVING (¼ CUP): 110 calories, 6 grams protein, 7 grams fat, 5 grams carbohydrates, 70 milligrams sodium, 0 milligrams cholesterol.

SERVING SUGGESTIONS: Serve this sauce with Roasted Eggplant Calzone (page 74), over grilled fish such as swordfish, or with pasta and vegetables.

Roasted Red Pepper Coulis

*R*oasting peppers gives them a whole new flavor— smoky, rich, and surprisingly sweet. If you have a lot of peppers to peel, try grilling them on a gas or charcoal grill for an extra level of flavor.

Makes approximately 1 cup (about 4 servings)

4 red bell peppers, halved and seeded	¼ cup heavy cream
1 to 2 tablespoons oil, or as needed	¼ teaspoon salt, or to taste
½ cup chicken broth (page 193) or vegetable broth (page 192), or as needed	¼ teaspoon freshly ground black pepper, or to taste

1. Preheat the oven to 450 degrees F. Rub the peppers lightly with oil and place cut side down on a baking sheet. Roast them in the preheated oven for 15 to 20 minutes, or until very soft. The skin should darken and pucker.

2. Transfer the peppers to a plastic bag and twist shut; set aside to cool for several minutes. Pull off skins and discard.

3. Purée the peppers in a food processor or blender, slowly adding the broth until the sauce is quite smooth and thin enough to pour easily.

4. Strain the mixture into a saucepan and add the heavy cream, salt, and pepper. Simmer for 2 to 3 minutes.

5. The coulis can be used immediately or stored in the refrigerator, covered, for up to 1 week.

NUTRITION INFORMATION, PER SERVING (¼ CUP): 80 calories, 2 grams protein, 6 grams fat, 5 grams carbohydrates, 145 milligrams sodium, 25 milligrams cholesterol.

PREPARATION NOTE: If you have a bumper crop of peppers available, multiply the recipe, and keep the coulis frozen for up to 2 months.

LOWER-FAT VERSION: Substitute canned evaporated skim milk for the heavy cream.

SERVING SUGGESTIONS: This sauce may be served as is or used to flavor tomato-based sauces, soups, or braised or stewed foods.

CORN RELISH

*W*hen corn season first arrives, most of us want nothing more than fresh ears, steamed, boiled, or roasted. But as the weeks go by, and the last corn is harvested, other preparations bring new, delicious dishes to our meals. This one also captures the sweet, robust taste to savor when the fields are buried under snow.

MAKES 1½ CUPS

2	ears corn, husked and silk removed		3	tablespoons cider vinegar
¼	cup diced red pepper		½	tablespoon powdered dry mustard
1	small jalapeño, seeded and finely chopped			Dash of Tabasco or similar hot pepper sauce
1	scallion, thinly sliced		1	teaspoon Worcestershire sauce, or to taste
2	tablespoons tightly packed brown sugar		½	teaspoon salt, or to taste

1. Steam or boil the corn 3 to 5 minutes, or until the kernels are just tender. Cut the kernels from the cob into a mixing bowl. Add the red pepper, jalapeño pepper, and scallion.

2. Heat the remaining ingredients in a skillet over high heat and bring to a boil. Add the corn mixture and toss just until evenly coated.

3. Serve the relish warm, or allow it to cool to room temperature; place it in a clean bowl or jar, cover tightly, and store in the refrigerator for up to 10 days. For longer storage, follow the preserving directions in Preparation Notes for Half-Sour Pickles (page 138).

NUTRITION INFORMATION, PER SERVING (ABOUT 3 TABLESPOONS): 65 calories, 2 grams protein, 1 gram fat, 15 grams carbohydrates, 170 milligrams sodium, 0 milligrams cholesterol.

PREPARATION NOTES: This relish can be made with flash-frozen corn kernels. The recipe can be doubled, tripled, or even quadrupled.

SERVING SUGGESTIONS: This lightly spiced, sweet and sour relish is a classic choice to accompany grilled hamburgers or steaks, hot dogs, or sandwiches. It can also be served on a bed of lettuce, with other sliced, shredded, or diced vegetables, such as cucumbers, carrots, jícama, bell peppers, celery, and radishes, to make a more substantial salad.

HALF-SOUR PICKLES

*P*ickling cucumbers, also known as Kirby cucumbers, can be found at many greengroceries and farm stands from the middle to the end of the summer. They are smaller and more "warty" than the slicing cucumbers used in salads and they are not normally waxed.

MAKES 25 PICKLES

1	tablespoon pickling spice	12	garlic cloves, peeled and crushed
½	cup cider vinegar	25	small pickling cucumbers, washed
1½	quarts water	3	sprigs fresh dill
¼	cup kosher salt		

1. Combine the pickling spice, vinegar, water, salt, garlic, and cucumbers in a stockpot and bring to a boil.

2. Remove the pan from the heat; remove the garlic and add the fresh dill.

3. Allow the pickles to marinate in the brine at least overnight. Serve when the flavor is fully developed. To put up the pickles, follow the instructions below.

NUTRITION INFORMATION, PER PICKLE: 12 calories, trace of protein, trace of fat, 2 grams carbohydrates, 1,000 milligrams sodium, 0 milligrams cholesterol.

PREPARATION NOTES: To put up the pickles, return the pickles and brine to a simmer. Remove the pickles and the dill with a slotted spoon and pack into hot sterilized jars to within 1 inch of the top. Return the liquid to a full boil, and pour it over the pickles to within ½ inch of the top of the jar. Seal the jars with sterilized lids, and place them in a boiling water bath for 15 minutes. Remove the jars and cool at room temperature; label and date the jars, and store in a cool, dry place.

SERVING SUGGESTIONS: This snappy pickle can be served any time as a low-fat and low-calorie snack, but it is a classic accompaniment to sandwiches of all sorts.

PICKLED BEETS AND ONIONS

The beets turn the onions a beautiful magenta, making this relish an eye-catching side dish or chilled salad.

MAKES 4 SERVINGS

16	baby beets, tops trimmed		⅓	cup white vinegar
2	medium red onions, julienned		2	teaspoons salt
2	tablespoons sugar		⅔	cup water

1. Place the beets in a pan and add enough cool water to cover by at least 2 inches. Simmer the beets over medium heat about 15 minutes, or until just tender. Drain and rinse under cold water; drain well. When the beets are cool enough to handle, slip off the skins and set them aside in a bowl.

2. Combine the onions, sugar, vinegar, salt, and water in a saucepan, and bring to a boil over high heat. Lower the heat and simmer, uncovered for 5 minutes.

3. Pour the hot onion mixture over the beets, and allow them to cool to room temperature. Cover the beets well and chill thoroughly for several hours or overnight before serving. The pickled beets may be stored in the refrigerator for up to 5 days.

NUTRITION INFORMATION, PER SERVING (ABOUT ¾ CUP): 80 calories, 2 grams protein, trace of fat, 20 grams carbohydrates, 1,065 milligrams sodium, 0 milligrams cholesterol.

PREPARATION NOTE: Eight medium beets can be substituted for the baby beets. Cut into wedges or slices after they are fully cooked.

VARIATION: Make pickled eggs by adding hard-boiled eggs to the marinade after it has cooled to room temperature. The eggs should marinate in the refrigerator at least 24 hours. They can then be quartered and served with the beets as a salad, or eaten whole.

SERVING SUGGESTIONS: This pickle can be served as part of a relish tray on a buffet or as an hors d'oeuvre plate to nibble with cocktails or aperitifs.

MANGO-BOURBON BARBECUE SAUCE

The combination of flavors in this barbecue sauce gives it a sweet, exotic flavor with Asian overtones. It is excellent with a variety of meats, especially pork and chicken, and can also be brushed on vegetable kebabs as they are grilled or broiled.

MAKES ABOUT 3 CUPS

1 tablespoon vegetable oil	2 ancho chiles, stems and seeds removed, chopped
1 onion, minced	
4 garlic cloves, chopped	2 tablespoons brown sugar, lightly packed
1¾ cups ketchup	
1 cup chicken broth (page 193)	2 tablespoons fresh lemon juice
1 cup diced fresh mango	1 tablespoon Worcestershire sauce
½ cup hoisin sauce	1 teaspoon grated lemon zest
½ cup cider vinegar	½ teaspoon Old Bay seafood seasoning
¼ cup bourbon	Freshly ground black pepper to taste
	Dash of cayenne pepper

1. Heat the oil over medium-high heat. Add the onions and garlic, and sauté for about 6 minutes, or until the onions are tender and have a sweet aroma.

2. Add the remaining ingredients and simmer for 1 hour.

3. Let the sauce cool slightly, then purée in a blender until very smooth. Use at once or cool and store in the refrigerator for up to 2 weeks.

NUTRITION INFORMATION, PER SERVING: 75 calories, 1 gram protein, 1 gram fat, 15 grams carbohydrates, 445 milligrams sodium, 0 milligrams cholesterol.

PREPARATION NOTE: A single mango will yield more than a cup when diced. Add the extra fruit to a green or fruit salad.

Bread

PUMPKIN BREAD

*T*his recipe produces a dense, moist bread that delivers the heady aroma and flavor of a pumpkin pie.

MAKES 2 LOAVES

1½	cups all-purpose flour
1	cup whole-wheat flour
½	teaspoon salt
1	teaspoon double-acting baking powder
¾	teaspoon baking soda
½	teaspoon ground cinnamon
¼	teaspoon freshly grated nutmeg

⅛	teaspoon ground cloves
½	cup raisins, plumped (page 191)
1	cup puréed cooked pumpkin (fresh, canned, or frozen)
¾	cup sugar
2	eggs
½	cup vegetable oil

1. Preheat the oven to 375 degrees F. Grease and flour two 8 ½ x 4 ½-inch loaf pans.
2. Sift together the flours, salt, baking powder, baking soda, cinnamon, nutmeg, and cloves.
3. Combine the raisins, pumpkin, sugar, eggs, and oil in a large bowl, and mix well.
4. Stir the dry ingredients into the pumpkin mixture all at once, and mix just until the dry ingredients are blended into the batter. Transfer the batter to the prepared loaf pans and bake in the preheated oven for 50 to 55 minutes.
5. Let the breads cool in the pans for 10 to 15 minutes, then ease them out of the pans and continue to cool on a rack.

Preceding Page: Pumpkin Bread

NUTRITION INFORMATION, PER 1-INCH-THICK SLICE: 200 calories, 3 grams protein, 10 grams fat, 26 grams carbohydrates, 160 milligrams sodium, 35 milligrams cholesterol.

VARIATION: Add ½ cup chopped toasted walnuts (page 192) to the batter.

SERVING SUGGESTIONS: This is a good bread to serve with a main-course salad, or on its own at breakfast with cream cheese.

BOSTON BROWN BREAD

*T*raditionally this bread was steamed in a covered kettle on top of the stove. With its molasses tang, moist dense texture, and cornmeal flavor, it is a fine accompaniment to hearty dishes like baked beans, pot roast, and stews.

MAKES ONE 6-SLICE LOAF

½	cup all-purpose flour		½	teaspoon salt
½	cup whole-wheat flour		1	egg
½	cup rye flour		½	cup dark molasses
½	cup cornmeal		1½	cups buttermilk
¾	teaspoon baking soda			

1. Preheat the oven to 375 degrees F. Generously grease a 9 x 5-inch loaf pan or a 1-pound coffee can.

2. Into a large mixing bowl sift the all-purpose flour, whole-wheat flour, rye flour, cornmeal, baking soda, and salt.

3. In a separate bowl, beat together the egg, molasses, and buttermilk.

4. Make a well in the center of the flour. Pour the liquid mixture into the well and mix until the batter is smooth. Transfer the batter to the prepared loaf pan or coffee can.

5. Cover the pan or can tightly with foil, then place it inside a larger baking pan (the sides of the larger pan should reach above the loaf pan or can). Pour enough boiling water into the large baking pan to come half-way up the sides of the loaf pan. Tightly cover the larger pan with foil and place in the preheated oven. Bake for 2½ hours; do not disturb or check during this time or the bread will not cook properly. When a skewer inserted into the center of the bread comes out clean, the bread is done; if it is not, re-cover with foil and continue to bake for 15 to 20 minutes longer.

6. When the bread is done, remove it from the steaming pan and remove the foil. Let it cool in the loaf pan or can for 10 minutes, then loosen around the edges, turn out, and cool slightly on a rack. Serve while still warm.

NUTRITION INFORMATION, PER SLICE: 265 calories, 8 grams protein, 2 grams fat, 55 grams carbohydrates, 730 milligrams sodium, 38 milligrams cholesterol.

Navajo Fry Bread

*T*his bread has been one of the most popular selections from the bread basket offered at The American Bounty since the doors first opened in 1982. The dough can be tricky to handle, since it is quite stiff when properly made. If you have one, a pasta machine can be a big help in rolling it out. In any case, it is important to allow the full time for the dough to rise, which will make it easier to roll out.

MAKES 2 "LOAVES" (ABOUT 6 TO 8 SERVINGS)

3 ¼	cups all-purpose flour	5	tablespoons plus 1 cup lard
1	cup dry powdered milk	1	cup ice water
1	tablespoon baking powder		Kosher or sea salt (optional)
½	teaspoon salt		

1. Stir together the flour, milk powder, baking powder, and salt.

2. Cut 5 tablespoons of the lard into the dry ingredients until the mixture has the consistency of coarse cornmeal.

3. Add the ice water and mix until the dough pulls cleanly away from the sides of the bowl. Cover the bowl with a towel and set the dough aside to rest at room temperature for 2 hours.

4. Divide the dough in half and shape each piece into a ball. Roll each piece out on a lightly floured work surface to a thickness of about ¼ inch.

5. Make 2 or 3 parallel cuts through the dough, but do not cut all the way to the edges. Let the dough rest briefly.

6. Heat about ½ of the remaining lard in a cast-iron skillet over medium-high heat. When the lard is very hot—a 1-inch cube of bread will brown in about 45 seconds—add the first shaped dough to the pan; fry for 4 to 5 minutes on the first side, until golden brown, then turn the bread and finish cooking on the second side, another 3 to 4 minutes.

7. Remove the bread from the skillet and drain on paper towels. Sprinkle with the salt. Keep the bread warm while frying the second round.

8. Cut the bread into wedges or break pieces away from the rounds at the table. Serve immediately, while still very warm.

NUTRITIONAL INFORMATION, PER SERVING: 275 calories, 7 grams protein, 13 grams fat, 31 grams carbohydrates, 240 milligrams sodium, 15 milligrams cholesterol.

VARIATION: Add up to 2 tablespoons of minced fresh herbs, such as rosemary, thyme, or sage to the dough.

LOWER-FAT VERSION: Replace the lard with vegetable oil. (This will give the bread a different taste.)

ZUCCHINI BREAD

There is a time of year when it seems that zucchini plants have become almost demonic in their ability to produce and produce. Zucchini bread is just one of the recipes developed over the years to accommodate a glut of this quick-growing summer squash.

MAKES 2 LOAVES

3½	cups all-purpose flour	2	large zucchini, grated (2½ cups)
1	teaspoon salt	1	cup sugar
2	teaspoons baking powder	4	eggs
½	teaspoon baking soda	½	cup vegetable oil
½	teaspoon ground cinnamon	1	cup chopped toasted walnuts or pecans
½	teaspoon freshly grated nutmeg		(page 192)
¼	teaspoon ground cloves		

1. Preheat the oven to 350 degrees. Grease and flour two 8½ x 4½-inch loaf pans.
2. Sift together the flour, salt, baking powder, baking soda, cinnamon, nutmeg, and cloves.
3. Combine the zucchini, sugar, eggs and oil in a large bowl and mix well.
4. Stir the sifted dry ingredients into the zucchini mixture just until the dry ingredients are blended into the batter. Fold in the nuts.
5. Transfer the batter to the prepared loaf pans.
6. Bake in the preheated oven for 50 to 55 minutes, then remove the breads from the pans and cool on racks.

NUTRITION INFORMATION, PER 1-INCH-THICK SLICE: 220 calories, 4 grams protein, 10 grams fat, 29 grams carbohydrates, 155 milligrams sodium, 45 milligrams cholesterol.

VARIATION: Reduce sugar to 3 tablespoons. Replace cinnamon, nutmeg, and cloves with ½ teaspoon each dried oregano, basil, and thyme. Replace ½ of the chopped nuts with ½ cup chopped rehydrated sun-dried tomatoes (page 191). Add up to ¼ cup chopped oil-cured olives.

Country-style Corn Bread

*C*onventional wisdom about what constitutes the "correct" way to make corn bread varies from one region of the country to another. Southerners tend to use little if any sugar in theirs, and often specify white cornmeal. In other parts of the country, yellow cornmeal is preferred, and the amount of sugar is noticeably increased.

MAKES 8 SERVINGS

1	cup cornmeal	1	teaspoon salt
¾	cup bread flour	2	eggs
1½	teaspoons baking powder	½	cup milk or buttermilk
½	cup sugar	¼	cup vegetable oil

1. Preheat the oven to 350 degrees F. Lightly oil a 9-inch square pan.
2. Mix together the cornmeal, bread flour, baking powder, sugar, and salt in a mixing bowl.
3. Stir together the eggs, buttermilk, and oil until blended.
4. Add the wet ingredients to the dry and combine until just mixed.
5. Pour the batter into the prepared pan and bake at 375 degrees F for 25 to 30 minutes, or until the surface is golden brown and it springs back when lightly pressed with a fingertip.
6. Cool the bread in the pan for about 10 minutes before cutting and serving.

NUTRITION INFORMATION, PER 2-INCH-SQUARE SERVING: 240 calories, 5 grams protein, 9 grams fat, 35 grams carbohydrates, 350 milligrams sodium, 70 milligrams cholesterol.

PREPARATION NOTES: To get a delicious, crisp bottom crust, bake the bread in a cast-iron skillet as follows: Place a 9-inch skillet in the oven as it preheats. When the batter is ready, remove the skillet from the oven and brush the inside lightly with oil or rendered bacon fat. Pour in the batter, and bake the bread as directed.

SERVING SUGGESTIONS: Serve this bread while it is still quite warm. It does not keep well, but leftovers can be made into bread crumbs and used in stuffing.

Overleaf: Country-style Corn Bread, Chipotle Corn Squares (muffin variation)

ANADAMA BREAD

The story of how this bread got its name varies slightly from one version to another, but in essence, it appears that a fisherman from New England had a wife named Anna who never fixed anything other than cornmeal mush sweetened with molasses. One night, furious at her inadequate meal, he mixed it together with flour and yeast and put it in the oven to bake, all the while muttering, "Anna, damn 'er!"

MAKES 2 LOAVES

¾	cup boiling water		2	tablespoons vegetable oil
1	cup yellow cornmeal		4½ to 5	cups bread flour
1½	cups warm water		2	teaspoons salt
1	package dry yeast		1	egg
½	cup dark molasses		2	tablespoons milk

1. Stir together the boiling water and cornmeal in a small bowl until quite smooth. Stir well, then cool to room temperature.

2. Combine the warm water, yeast, and molasses in a large bowl; set aside for 2 to 3 minutes (the yeast will bubble and look frothy).

3. Add the oil, cooled cornmeal mixture, 2 cups of the bread flour, and the salt. Stir until a shaggy dough forms. Continue to stir, adding more flour as necessary, until the dough begins to form a ball that pulls cleanly away from the sides of the bowl.

4. Turn the dough onto a lightly floured work surface and knead for 10 minutes, adding only enough additional flour to prevent the dough from sticking. The dough should be moist, smooth, and springy.

5. Lightly grease a large bowl with a small amount of oil. Place the dough in the bowl, cover with a clean towel, and place in a warm, draft-free spot to rise for 1½ to 2 hours, or until double in volume. While the dough is rising, prepare two 9-inch loaf pans by lightly buttering or oiling them.

6. Punch the dough down and divide it in half. Shape the dough into loaves and place them in the prepared bread pans. Cover with the towel and let rise again for 45 minutes to an hour, or until nearly double in volume. Preheat the oven to 375 degrees F.

7. Beat together the egg and milk. Brush the tops of the loaves with this egg wash, and bake in the preheated oven for 35 minutes or until golden brown (the loaves should make a slightly hollow sound when lightly rapped on the bottom with a knuckle). Remove the loaves from the oven and cool in the pans for 3 minutes, then ease the loaves out of the pans and place them on a rack to complete cooling.

NUTRITION INFORMATION, PER 1-INCH-THICK SLICE: 120 calories, 3 grams protein, 2 grams fat, 22 grams carbohydrates, 205 milligrams sodium, 0 milligrams cholesterol.

PREPARATION NOTES: Yeast breads require time for rising and baking, but they can be manipulated to fit your schedule. The bread can be mixed and kneaded, then left to rise very slowly in the refrigerator for about 12 hours. Bring the dough back to room temperature before shaping and baking.

SERVING SUGGESTIONS: This bread makes excellent French toast. Mix together 1 cup of milk with 1 or 2 eggs, a dash of cinnamon, and a teaspoon of sugar. Dip the sliced bread in this custard mixture and pan-fry in a lightly oiled skillet or griddle over medium-high heat. Top with maple syrup and toasted nuts (page 192).

BASIC FLATBREAD

*T*his recipe is for a type of bread dough that baker's would refer to as "lean." It is among the simplest of bread recipes, containing very little beyond the most basic breadmaking requirements: flour, yeast, water, and salt.

MAKES 4 PORTIONS

1	package dry yeast	2 to 2½	cups bread flour
1½	cups warm water	2	teaspoons kosher salt
2	tablespoons honey	1	tablespoon chopped fresh rosemary,
4	tablespoons olive oil		chives or basil (optional)
2	cups whole-wheat flour		Cornmeal

1. Rinse a clean bowl with warm water, dry and oil it lightly.
2. Stir together the yeast and ½ cup of the warm water in a mixing bowl and let stand for 10 minutes, or until a thick foam develops.
3. Add the remaining warm water, honey, and half of the oil; stir to blend.
4. Add the whole-wheat flour, 1 cup of bread flour, the salt, and the herbs (if desired) to the yeast mixture. Stir well for about 5 minutes.
5. Continue to add flour to the dough until a smooth, heavy dough forms.
6. Turn the dough out of the bowl onto a floured surface and knead for several minutes, adding more flour as necessary to prevent sticking. The dough should feel very smooth, elastic, and springy.
7. Place the dough in the oiled bowl, cover with a towel, and allow to rise in a warm, draft-free spot until doubled in volume, 1 to 1½ hours.
8. Punch the dough down and divide it into 4 balls. Roll and stretch the dough into circles about ¼-inch thick.
9. Sprinkle cookie sheets with cornmeal. Place the shaped dough on the sheets, cover, and let rise for 30 minutes. Preheat the oven to 425 degrees F.
10. Brush the dough with the remaining olive oil and bake for approximately 15 minutes or until golden brown and puffed.

NUTRITION INFORMATION, PER SERVING: 280 calories, 7 grams protein, 5 grams fat, 50 grams carbohydrates, 360 milligrams sodium, 0 milligrams cholesterol.

PREPARATION NOTES: This recipe can be doubled. To freeze the dough, prepare it through step 8. Wrap each piece of dough in freezer paper. To use frozen dough, allow it to thaw in the refrigerator overnight. Let it come to room temperature for 45 minutes or so before shaping and baking.

SERVING SUGGESTIONS: This dough is used to prepare flatbreads, pizzas, calzones, or focaccia. It can be grilled rather than baked, and served while still very hot with a bowl of extra-virgin olive oil and sea salt to be added by each person according to taste.

Flatbread with Tomatoes, Rosemary, Garlic, and Monterey Jack Cheese

*F*latbread might be familiar to many people as a thin, unleavened bread, quite like a cracker in texture. This version is indebted to an Italian tradition of yeast-leavened breads baked flat, some without a topping, some with, as here.

MAKES 4 PORTIONS

1 recipe plain or herb-flavored flatbread dough (page 152)	2 tablespoons chopped fresh rosemary
Cornmeal	2 red beefsteak tomatoes, sliced
¼ cup extra-virgin olive oil	10 dry-cured Greek black olives, pitted
¼ cup minced garlic	½ cup freshly grated dry Monterey Jack or Parmesan cheese

1. Prepare the flatbread dough through step 7 and set aside to rise while preparing the topping.
2. Preheat the oven to 425 degrees F. Scatter an 11 x 15-inch baking sheet with a light layer of cornmeal.
3. Heat the olive oil in a small pan over medium heat. Add the garlic and cook gently until it has a sweet, roasted aroma, about 4 minutes. Remove the pan from the heat and add the rosemary. Set aside to steep while shaping the dough.
4. Roll or stretch the dough into a large rectangle, and transfer it to the prepared baking sheet. Dimple the surface with your fingertips.
5. Brush the shaped dough with the garlic-rosemary oil mixture; reserve the extra oil.
6. Arrange tomatoes and olives on the surface and sprinkle evenly with cheese.
7. Bake the flatbread on the bottom rack of the preheated oven until the crust is golden and the cheese has lightly browned, 12 to 16 minutes.
8. Drizzle the remaining rosemary-garlic oil over the top, and serve at once.

NUTRITION INFORMATION, PER 3-INCH-SQUARE SERVING: 620 calories, 17 grams protein, 37 grams fat, 53 grams carbohydrates, 680 milligrams sodium, 40 milligrams cholesterol.

PREPARATION NOTES: The flatbread dough may be prepared in advance and then held, tightly covered, in the refrigerator for up to 18 hours. Allow the dough about 45 minutes to return to room temperature before shaping it.

VARIATIONS: Additional fresh herbs could be added to the dough, before it is kneaded, to intensify the flavor in the finished flatbread.

Other toppings could be used in place of or in addition to those suggested: strips of roasted bell peppers or thinly sliced red onion; crumbled goat cheese, or slivers of country-style ham. Alternate slices of red and yellow tomatoes for greater visual appeal.

SERVING SUGGESTIONS: Flatbread can be served as part of a light meal, with soups, or as a first course or with drinks.

CHIPOTLE CORN SQUARES

*T*he addition of smoky, roasted jalapeños and some of the rich sauce they are canned in results in a perfect corn bread to serve with hearty soups or chili.

MAKES 8 SERVINGS

1	cup all-purpose flour		1	egg
1	cup yellow cornmeal		¼	cup vegetable oil
¼	cup sugar		2	teaspoons chopped, canned chipotle
2	teaspoons baking powder			peppers, including juices and sauce
½	teaspoon salt		¼	cup diced red pepper
½	cup corn kernels, fresh or frozen		¼	cup diced green pepper
1	cup milk			

1. Preheat the oven to 350 degrees F. Lightly grease a 9-inch-square baking pan.

2. Place the flour, cornmeal, sugar, baking powder, and salt in a mixing bowl, and stir until all ingredients are evenly distributed; make a well in the center.

3. Combine the corn kernels, milk, egg, oil, and peppers in a separate bowl. Stir together with a fork until evenly blended.

4. Pour the wet ingredients into the well in the dry ingredients and mix the batter just until it is evenly moistened. The batter may still appear a bit lumpy.

5. Pour the batter into the prepared pan and bake in the preheated oven until a toothpick inserted into the bread comes out clean, about 35 minutes.

6. Allow the corn bread to cool slightly before cutting it into squares. Serve while still warm.

NUTRITION INFORMATION, PER 3-INCH-SQUARE SERVING: 160 calories, 3 grams protein, 6 grams fat, 23 grams carbohydrates, 175 milligrams sodium, 20 milligrams cholesterol.

PREPARATION NOTES: To get a delicious, crisp bottom crust, bake the bread in a cast-iron skillet as follows: Place a 9-inch skillet in the oven as it preheats. When the batter is ready, remove the skillet from the oven and brush the inside lightly with oil or rendered bacon fat. Pour in the batter, and bake the bread as directed.

VARIATIONS: Canned green chiles can be substituted for chipotles (for a milder taste) or chopped fresh jalapeños (for more heat). About ½ cup of grated sharp Cheddar cheese can be folded into the batter, or scattered over the top before baking.

To cut the corn bread into diamonds, first make an initial cut that runs from the upper left-hand corner of the pan diagonally to the bottom right-hand corner. Then, make more cuts, parallel to the first one, about 3 inches apart. Repeat this sequence, cutting first from the upper right-hand corner to the lower left-hand corner.

The batter also can be poured into greased or paper-lined muffin pans and baked for 20 to 25 minutes.

SERVING SUGGESTION: Serve with Seafood Gumbo (page 50).

PARKER HOUSE ROLLS

*T*hese rolls gained fame at one of Boston's hotels, the Parker House. Delicately textured and rich with butter, they are perhaps the quintessential Sunday dinner roll.

MAKES ABOUT 2 DOZEN ROLLS

⅓	cup warm water	2½ to 3	cups bread flour
1	package dry yeast	1	teaspoon salt
2	tablespoons sugar	½	cup melted butter (or more as needed)
3	eggs	2	tablespoons milk
¾	cup milk, scalded and cooled		
3	tablespoons unsalted butter, at room temperature		

1. Combine the warm water, yeast, and sugar in a large bowl and stir well. Set aside for 2 to 3 minutes or until quite frothy.

2. Lightly beat 2 eggs and add them to the yeast with the milk, butter, 1½ cups of the flour, and the salt. Stir well for several minutes until the dough begins to form long elastic strands. Add more flour gradually until the dough is too heavy to stir.

3. Turn the dough onto a lightly floured work surface, and knead for about 10 minutes, adding enough flour to prevent the dough from sticking. The dough should be moist, smooth, and springy.

4. Place the dough in a large, lightly oiled bowl, cover with a clean cloth, and allow to rise in a warm, draft-free spot for 1 to 2 hours or until double in volume. Lightly grease two 9 x 13-inch baking dishes.

5. Punch the dough down and flatten to about a 1-inch thickness. Cut the dough into rectangles, about 1 inch by 2 inches. Press the dull side of a table knife into the center of each rectangle to make a crease.

6. Brush the rectangles with a thin coating of melted butter, and fold the dough over so that the butter is on the inside.

7. Place the rolls into the prepared pans. They should be close, but not touching one another. Cover the shaped rolls and let them rise until nearly doubled. Preheat the oven to 350 degrees F.

8. Beat the remaining egg with the milk. Brush the rolls lightly with egg wash and bake them in the preheated oven for 15 to 20 minutes or until golden brown and baked through. Let the rolls cool slightly before serving.

NUTRITION INFORMATION, PER ROLL: 113 calories, 3 grams protein, 5 grams fat, 14 grams carbohydrates, 150 milligrams sodium, 33 milligrams cholesterol.

PREPARATION NOTES: This dough can be left to rise very slowly in a cool spot, or overnight in the refrigerator. Let the dough return to room temperature before final shaping and baking.

VARIATION: Sesame or poppy seeds can be scattered over the rolls after they have been brushed with egg wash.

SERVING SUGGESTIONS: These buttery rolls are at their best when served warm. They are great with a special family dinner, or with big cups of frothy cappuccino or hot chocolate for breakfast.

SMOKED PROVOLONE AND THYME MUFFINS

*T*hese muffins are one of the newest additions to The American Bounty's bread basket, and they are fast becoming the most frequently requested selection. They can be easily varied by substituting other cheeses and herbs, or by adding ingredients such as those suggested in the notes following the method.

MAKES 12 MUFFINS

2	cups all-purpose flour		Pinch of cayenne pepper
1	cup grated smoked provolone cheese	1	egg
1	tablespoon baking powder	2	tablespoons dry mustard
1	tablespoon chopped fresh thyme,	1½	cups milk
	or 2 teaspoons dried	¼	cup butter, melted and cooled
½	teaspoon kosher salt		Dash of Tabasco or similar hot pepper
	Freshly ground black pepper to taste		sauce to taste

1. Preheat the oven to 350 degrees F. Spray or brush muffin tins lightly with oil, or use paper liners.
2. Stir together the flour, cheese, baking powder, thyme, salt, and pepper in a large mixing bowl; make a well in the center.
3. Blend the egg, dry mustard, milk, butter, and hot sauce in a separate bowl.
4. Pour the wet ingredients into the well in the dry ingredients. Stir together the wet and dry ingredients, mixing just until all ingredients are combined. Do not overmix.
5. Spoon the batter into the muffin tins, filling them three-quarters full.
6. Bake the muffins in the preheated oven for 20 to 25 minutes or until the tops spring back when lightly pressed with a fingertip.
7. Cool the muffins in the tin for about 10 minutes, then turn them out of the pan. Serve while still warm.

NUTRITION INFORMATION, PER MUFFIN: 175 calories, 6 grams protein, 9 grams fat, 17 grams carbohydrates, 310 milligrams sodium, 50 milligrams cholesterol.

VARIATIONS: Smoked mozzarella, aged cheddar, Monterey Jack (plain or peppered), or smoked Gouda make good substitutes for the provolone. Chives, basil, oregano, or marjoram can be used in place of the thyme.

PREPARATION NOTES: If the muffins are made ahead of time, refresh them by briefly reheating in a 250-degree F oven. The freshly baked muffins can be cooled to room temperature, transferred to a freezer bag, and frozen for up to 8 weeks. To serve, thaw at room temperature, then reheat in a warm oven.

SERVING SUGGESTIONS: These muffins can be served on their own as an appetizer or a snack along with beer or wine at an informal gathering. For mini-muffins, cut the baking time to 10 to 12 minutes.

BLUEBERRY MUFFINS

S ometimes blueberries turn a peculiar green color as they bake in cakes or muffins. This happens in batters that include buttermilk and baking soda and is the result of acids interacting with the berry. In this recipe, whole milk and baking powder are used and the result is tender muffins with a good rise and rich, purple-colored berries.

MAKES 1 DOZEN MUFFINS

2	cups plus 2 tablespoons all-purpose flour	½	cup sugar
1½	teaspoons double-acting baking powder	1	egg
½	teaspoon salt	½	cup milk
¼	teaspoon freshly grated nutmeg	½	teaspoon vanilla extract
¼	cup butter, at room temperature	2	cups blueberries, picked over, washed and patted dry

1. Preheat the oven to 400 degrees F. Use paper liners or grease and flour a muffin pan.
2. Sift together 2 cups of the flour, baking powder, salt, and nutmeg.
3. Cream together the butter and sugar until very light. Mix in the egg, milk, and vanilla.
4. Add the dry ingredients to the liquid mixture all at once, and stir until they are just blended.
5. Toss the blueberries with the remaining two tablespoons of flour. Fold the blueberries gently into the batter.
6. Fill each muffin cup two-thirds full with batter. Bake in the preheated oven for 18 to 20 minutes, or until the top of the muffin springs back when lightly pressed.
7. Cool in the pan for 5 minutes; remove and cool on a rack.

NUTRITION INFORMATION, PER MUFFIN: 195 calories, 3 grams protein, 9 grams fat, 26 grams carbohydrates, 170 milligrams sodium, 39 milligrams cholesterol.

AHEAD OF TIME: These muffins can be frozen and thawed at room temperature for an hour, then warmed in a 250-degree F oven for several minutes.

VARIATIONS: Unsweetened frozen berries can be used. Frozen berries need not be thawed, but baking time may increase by as much as 3 minutes.

CHEDDAR BISCUITS

Sharp, aged, farm-style Cheddar cheeses, white or yellow, are best for these biscuits. Yellow cheddar will give the biscuits a deeper golden color.

MAKES 1 DOZEN BISCUITS

1	teaspoon fennel seeds (optional)	½	teaspoon salt
3	cups all-purpose flour	½	cup shortening or butter, cut into dice
1	tablespoon sugar	¾	cup cold milk
1	tablespoon baking powder	1	cup grated Cheddar cheese

1. Preheat the oven to 400 degrees F. Soak the fennel seeds in warm water for 15 minutes, then drain and dry on paper towels.

2. Combine the flour, sugar, baking powder, and salt. Cut the shortening or butter into the flour until the mixture is the consistency of coarse cornmeal. Make a well in this mixture.

3. Add the milk, cheese, and fennel seeds, mixing with a fork just until the dough pulls away from the sides of the bowl.

4. Turn the dough onto a lightly floured work surface and knead gently 5 to 6 times. Do not overwork the dough. Roll the dough out into a ½-inch-thick rectangle; using a 2-inch round cutter, cut the dough into biscuits.

5. Place the biscuits on an ungreased baking sheet approximately 1 inch apart and bake in the preheated oven for 15 to 20 minutes, until golden brown.

NUTRITION INFORMATION, PER BISCUIT: 250 calories, 7 grams protein, 14 grams fat, 24 grams carbohydrates, 380 milligrams sodium, 60 milligrams cholesterol.

PREPARATION NOTES: Placing the biscuits 1 inch apart on the baking sheet will produce biscuits that have crisp-sided crust. For softer-sided biscuits, place them in a square baking pan with the sides nearly touching. The total baking time will increase by 5 to 10 minutes. Pull the biscuits apart to serve.

SERVING SUGGESTIONS: Spread some mustard on split biscuits and add some slivers of country-style ham or smoked turkey breast for a wonderful accompaniment to drinks.

ANGEL BISCUITS

*T*hese biscuits are reputedly as "light as an angel's kiss." Yeast gives them a less flaky, more toothsome texture than traditional baking powder biscuits, and buttermilk gives them a slight tang similar to the flavor that might be achieved with a sourdough starter.

MAKES 10 TO 12 BISCUITS

½ envelope dry yeast	½ teaspoon kosher salt
¼ cup warm water	1 cup buttermilk
2 ½ cups all-purpose flour	½ cup melted and cooled vegetable
½ tablespoon baking powder	shortening
½ teaspoon baking soda	1 egg white
2 tablespoons sugar	

1. Lightly oil a baking sheet.
2. Stir together the yeast and warm water in a small bowl and let stand for 5 minutes, or until foamy.
3. Combine the flour, baking powder, baking soda, sugar, and salt in another bowl, and stir to distribute ingredients evenly; make a well in the center.
4. Add the buttermilk and melted shortening to the yeast mixture and pour it into the well in the dry ingredients.
5. Quickly stir the ingredients just until the dough begins to form a heavy shaggy mass. Do not overmix.
6. Turn the dough out onto a well-floured surface and pat it into a square, then roll it out to about ½-inch thick with a rolling pin. Cut the dough into 2-inch circles using a biscuit cutter.
7. Place the biscuits about 1 inch apart on the baking sheet. Allow to rise slightly in a warm place, 35 to 45 minutes, or until nearly doubled in volume. Preheat the oven to 425 degrees F.
8. Whisk the egg white together with 1 tablespoon of cold water and brush the tops of each biscuit lightly with the mixture.
9. Bake until the tops of the biscuits are light brown, 15 to 18 minutes.
10. Remove the biscuits from the oven and cool slightly; serve while still warm.

NUTRITION INFORMATION, PER BISCUIT: 190 calories, 4 grams protein, 8 grams fat, 23 grams carbohydrates, 160 milligrams sodium, 1 milligram cholesterol.

PREPARATION NOTES: This dough can be prepared through step 6, but not rolled out, and then left to rise in the refrigerator overnight, or up to 12 hours. Allow the dough to warm at room temperature for about 20 minutes before baking.

SERVING SUGGESTIONS: These are a delicious accompaniment to any meal, but they also are good served on their own with fresh butter, a pot of honey or jam, and a steaming mug of tea. Or spread them with some of Heywood's Mustard (page 132) and top with thin slices of country-style ham or leftover grilled steak.

JALAPEÑO BISCUITS

*A*mong the many chile varieties showing up in produce sections nationwide are jalapeños. Look for green glossy jalapeños that feel heavy for their size.

MAKES 12 BISCUITS

2	cups all-purpose flour
1	tablespoon baking powder
¾	teaspoon salt
5	tablespoons vegetable shortening
½ to ¾	cup buttermilk

½	jalapeño pepper, seeded and minced (or more to taste)
	Cracked freshly ground black pepper to taste

1. Preheat the oven to 400 degrees F. Lightly grease a cookie sheet.
2. Sift the flour, baking powder, and salt together into a mixing bowl or the bowl of a food processor.
3. Cut in the shortening until the mixture looks like coarse meal.
4. Add ½ cup of the buttermilk and stir or process until just blended. Gradually add more buttermilk as needed to make a heavy dough.
5. Turn the dough out onto a well-floured work surface. Knead lightly.
6. Roll the dough out to a ½-inch-thick rectangle.
7. Sprinkle half the dough with the minced jalapeño and black pepper; fold the dough in half.
8. Roll the dough lengthwise to ½-inch thickness to seal in peppers. Cut the dough into 2-inch circles.
9. Arrange the circles about ½ inch apart on a greased cookie sheet and bake for 10 to 15 minutes, until golden brown on top. Serve the biscuits hot from the oven.

NUTRITION INFORMATION, PER BISCUIT: 120 calories, 2 grams protein, 5 grams fat, 16 grams carbohydrates, 195 milligrams sodium, 8 milligrams cholesterol.

PREPARATION NOTE: Butter or lard may be substituted for the shortening for a more distinctive flavor.

SERVING SUGGESTIONS: Serve with grilled foods, particularly chicken, tuna, or swordfish; these also make a good "mop" for chili.

Desserts

PUMPKIN BREAD PUDDING

*T*his luscious pudding makes a fine change from traditional pumpkin pies as part of a holiday banquet. Whole-wheat bread along with the classic filling delivers the wonderful tastes of pumpkin pie, in a new package.

MAKES 8 SERVINGS

7 slices whole-grain bread, cubed	½ cup raisins
2 cups milk	½ teaspoon ground cinnamon
4 whole eggs	⅛ teaspoon ground cloves
1 cup sugar	⅛ teaspoon freshly grated nutmeg
1½ cups cooked, puréed pumpkin, fresh or canned	⅛ teaspoon ground allspice

1. Preheat the oven to 350 degrees F. Place the bread cubes on a baking sheet to toast for 10 to 12 minutes. Lightly butter a 2-quart casserole or baking dish.

2. Beat together the milk, eggs, and sugar in a large bowl until thoroughly blended.

3. Add the bread cubes to the mixture and stir to moisten evenly. Set aside for 15 minutes.

4. Combine the pumpkin, raisins, cinnamon, cloves, nutmeg, and allspice, and stir into the bread mixture. Pour into the prepared casserole and cover with foil or parchment paper.

5. Place the casserole in a larger baking pan, and add enough hot water to come up to the level of the pudding.

6. Bake in the preheated oven for 30 minutes. Remove the cover and continue baking for 15 minutes, or until the pudding is completely set and the top lightly browned.

NUTRITION INFORMATION, PER SERVING (¾ CUP): 267 calories, 7 grams protein, 6 grams fat, 51 grams carbohydrates, 180 milligrams sodium, 145 milligrams cholesterol.

AHEAD OF TIME: The mixture may be combined and set aside, in the refrigerator, for up to 2 hours; add about 10 minutes to the baking time.

VARIATION: The sugar can be replaced with ¾ cup maple syrup.

SERVING SUGGESTION: French Vanilla Ice Cream (page 172) is excellent with this.

Preceding Page: Pumpkin Bread Pudding

TRIPLE CHOCOLATE
PECAN BROWNIES

*T*hese brownies are loaded with nuts and chunks of white chocolate. For the best results, look for a good-quality white chocolate brand such as Vahlrona or Lindt.

MAKES 12 BROWNIES

5	ounces bittersweet chocolate	2	teaspoons vanilla extract
¾	cup (1½ sticks) unsalted butter	¾	cup all-purpose flour, sifted
⅔	cup Dutch-process cocoa powder	½	cup chopped, toasted pecans (page 192)
1½	cups granulated sugar	¾	cup (about 3 ounces) white chocolate,
3	eggs		roughly chopped

1. Preheat the oven to 375 degrees F. Butter and lightly flour a 9 x 13-inch baking pan.

2. Melt the bittersweet chocolate and butter in the top of a double boiler or in a microwave oven (20 to 40 seconds on high power).

3. Stir together the cocoa powder and sugar to break up any lumps in the cocoa. Blend the cocoa and sugar with the chocolate until the mixture is smooth.

4. Beat in the eggs and vanilla until thoroughly blended. Add the flour and stir until just combined.

5. Fold in the pecans and white chocolate, and pour the batter into the prepared baking pan.

6. Bake the brownies in the preheated oven until they have just barely shrunk away from the sides of the pan, 30 to 35 minutes.

7. Let the brownies cool to room temperature, then cut into bars.

NUTRITION INFORMATION, PER BAR: 450 calories, 5 grams protein, 33 grams fat, 41 grams carbohydrates, 54 milligrams sodium, 115 milligrams cholesterol.

VARIATIONS: The white chocolate and/or the nuts can be eliminated. Macadamia nuts, hazelnuts, or walnuts can be used in place of the pecans. Replace the white chocolate with equal amounts of peanut butter chips or M & M's.

LEMON POPPY SEED POUND CAKE

Poppy seeds give this finely textured cake a bit of crunch. The lemon syrup adds moisture, sheen, and an extra layer of lemon flavor. This cake is perfect for afternoon tea on the porch.

MAKES 1 BUNDT CAKE

½	cup milk	6	tablespoons poppy seeds
6	large eggs	1½	teaspoons baking powder
1	tablespoon vanilla extract	½	teaspoon salt
3	cups sifted cake flour	1	cup (2 sticks) butter, at room
2¼	cups sugar		temperature
2	loosely packed tablespoons lemon zest	½	cup fresh lemon juice

1. Lightly spray or wipe an 8-cup bundt pan with cooking oil. Preheat the oven to 350 degrees F.

2. Blend the milk, eggs, and vanilla together in a small bowl.

3. Place cake flour, 1½ cups of the sugar, lemon zest, poppy seeds, baking powder, and salt in the large bowl of an electric mixer; stir to combine.

4. Add the butter and half the egg mixture to the large bowl; mix on low speed just until the mixture is moistened.

5. Gradually add the remaining egg mixture in two batches, beating for 2 to 3 minutes after each addition.

6. Spoon the batter into the prepared bundt pan. Bake in the preheated oven for 45 to 50 minutes, or until a wooden tester comes out clean and the cake springs back from the touch.

7. Heat the remaining ¾ cup sugar and the lemon juice in a small saucepan over medium heat until the sugar dissolves, 3 to 4 minutes.

8. As soon as the cake comes out of the oven, place it on a cooling rack. Pierce the surface evenly with a wooden skewer, and brush repeatedly with the lemon syrup. Cool completely in the pan before removing the cake.

NUTRITION INFORMATION, PER 2-INCH SLICE: 455 calories, 10 grams protein, 22 grams fat, 60 grams carbohydrates, 354 milligrams sodium, 179 milligrams cholesterol.

VARIATIONS: This recipe can be used to prepare two 8-inch loaf cakes. The baking time will be reduced to 30 to 35 minutes. Or, line muffin tins with papers and fill two-thirds full to make 2 dozen cupcakes. Bake in a preheated oven for 20 to 25 minutes.

To make a lemon glaze, mix 1½ cups sifted confectioners' sugar with 2 tablespoons fresh lemon juice. Add boiling water a little at a time until a thick but pourable glaze forms. Set the cooled cake or cupcakes on a rack in a baking sheet and quickly pour or ladle the glaze over the tops.

SERVING SUGGESTION: This makes a wonderful addition to an afternoon tea party or coffee break.

French Vanilla Ice Cream

*T*his is the classic, all-American favorite—a rich, creamy ice cream flavored generously with vanilla. In some parts of the country this still is known as frozen custard, a particularly apt name, since it is based on a rich custard sauce.

MAKES ABOUT 1¼ QUARTS, OR 8 SERVINGS

4	cups half-and-half	1	vanilla bean split lengthwise
2	cups granulated sugar	6	egg yolks

1. Set a fine strainer over a medium bowl. Put about 2 inches of ice in a larger bowl, add enough water to cover the cubes, and set the medium bowl with the strainer into this ice bath.

2. Combine the half-and-half, 1½ cups of the sugar, and the vanilla bean in a heavy saucepan over medium heat and bring to a simmer, stirring constantly.

3. Whisk the egg yolks together with the remaining ½ cup sugar until thick and pale yellow.

4. Gradually whisk about 1½ cups of the hot half-and-half mixture into the beaten yolks. Transfer the yolk mixture to the saucepan and continue to cook over low heat, stirring constantly, until the custard coats the back of a spoon (about 180 degrees F on a candy or frying thermometer). Take care not to overheat the mixture or it will curdle.

5. Immediately strain the custard through a sieve into a bowl. Immediately refrigerate the custard. Stir every few minutes until it is quite cool.

6. Remove the vanilla pod and scrape out the seeds with a spoon; add the seeds to the custard.

7. Cover the custard and let it chill in the refrigerator for at least 4 hours or overnight. Freeze in an ice cream maker according to the manufacturer's instructions.

8. Pack the ice cream in plastic containers and freeze for several hours before serving.

NUTRITION INFORMATION, PER SERVING (4 OUNCES): 395 calories, 6 grams protein, 19 grams fat, 54 grams carbohydrates, 65 milligrams sodium, 250 milligrams cholesterol.

PREPARATION NOTES: When preparing vanilla ice cream, it is best to use a whole vanilla bean to get the fullest flavor. When preparing any of the following variations, however, 1 teaspoon of good-quality vanilla extract is just fine.

VARIATIONS:

CINNAMON: Add 2 cinnamon sticks to the half-and-half in step 2 and proceed as above.

NUT: Add 1 cup of toasted, chopped nuts (page 192) to the custard after straining. Almonds, macadamia nuts, pistachios, walnuts, or pecans are good choices.

PRALINE NUT: Toss the nuts in caramelized sugar (made by heating about ¼ cup of sugar, honey, or maple syrup until it is very thick and has a pronounced caramel aroma). Once coated, transfer the nuts to an oiled baking sheet, spread them in a layer, and let them cool completely before chopping and adding them to the ice cream.

PEACH OR APRICOT: Peel the fruit and cut it into slices or chunks; toss with a few tablespoons of granulated sugar to help the fruit release its juices. Allow the fruit to rest at room temperature for at least 1 hour before adding it to the custard after it has cooled and just before it is placed in the ice cream machine.

SERVING SUGGESTIONS: This ice cream is wonderful as a topping for Apple Pie (page 174), Triple Chocolate Pecan Brownies (page 169), or as an accompaniment to Berry Cobbler (page 186) or Spiced Pear Crisp (page 176).

APPLE PIE

*B*rimming with luscious fragrant fruit, this irresistable pie is the perfect example of "American bounty." Select an apple that is good for baking: Northern Spy, Rome Beauty, or Golden Delicious are good choices, but ask your greengrocer for other suggestions of other varieties available in your part of the country.

MAKES ONE 10-INCH PIE, 8 TO 10 SERVINGS

1 recipe Flaky Pie Dough (page 194)	¼ teaspoon freshly grated nutmeg
7 to 8 Rome Beauty apples	3 tablespoons butter, cut into small
1 teaspoon freshly squeezed lemon juice	pieces
¾ cup brown or white sugar	1 egg yolk mixed with 1 teaspoon of milk
4 tablespoons flour	or water, or plain milk
¾ teaspoon ground cinnamon	

1. Preheat the oven to 425 degrees F. Position a rack in the middle of the oven. Chill the pie dough according to recipe directions.

2. Peel, core, and slice the apples into a large bowl; sprinkle with lemon juice and toss gently.

3. Stir together the sugar, flour, cinnamon, and nutmeg. Add this mixture to the apples and toss to evenly coat all the slices with the spice mixture.

4. Divide the chilled dough in half; roll out the first half so that it will be large enough to overhang a 10-inch pie plate by 1 inch and fit it into the pie plate. Mound the apples in the pie shell, higher at the center than at the edges. Dot the top evenly with the butter.

5. Roll out the second half of the dough for the top crust and cut 2 or 3 vents into it or cut a small round from the center with a biscuit cutter. Lay the top crust over the apple filling, fold over the extra dough from the bottom, and crimp the edges together. Brush the top crust lightly with the egg and milk mixture or with plain milk.

6. Set the pie on the middle oven rack and place a sheet pan underneath to catch drips. Bake in the preheated oven for 15 minutes. Reduce the heat to 350 degrees F and continue to bake 30 to 40 minutes or until the apples feel tender when pierced through the steam vents with a knife and the crust is golden brown.

7. Remove the pie from the oven and cool it on a rack. Serve warm or at room temperature.

NUTRITION INFORMATION, PER SLICE: 516 calories, 3 grams protein, 22 grams fat, 78 grams carbohydrates, 391 milligrams sodium, 50 milligrams cholesterol.

PREPARATION NOTES: To decorate the pie, save any scraps left after trimming the dough to fit. Roll them out and cut into the desired shapes: leaves, apples, etc. Apply them to the top crust, after it has been brushed with the egg-milk mixture. Brush the tops of the decorations as well.

If desired, combine 1 tablespoon sugar with ½ teaspoon ground cinnamon and sprinkle evenly over the top of the pie after brushing with egg wash.

VARIATIONS: To make a deep-dish pie, pour the filling into a lightly greased 2½-inch-deep pie plate or 9-inch-square baking pan. Top with half the dough and bake as directed. Spoon the pie directly from the baking dish.

Add ½ cup plumped raisins or currants (page 191), or toasted nuts (page 192) for added texture and flavor.

This recipe also can be used to make pear, peach, plum, and apricot pies.

SERVING SUGGESTIONS: Accompanied by French Vanilla Ice Cream (page 172) or any good-quality prepared ice cream, this is a classic. But for a change, try a wedge of well-aged Cheddar cheese instead.

SPICED PEAR CRISP

*T*he range of fruit desserts popular throughout the country is staggering. Crisps have a sweet, crumbly upper layer; this one is made with oats.

MAKES 6 TO 8 SERVINGS

8	medium pears (Bartlett or Comice), peeled, cored, and thickly sliced	½	cup flour
½	cup brown sugar	½	cup rolled quick-cooking oatmeal
1	tablespoon lemon juice	½	cup chopped, toasted almonds, walnuts, or pecans (page 192)
1	teaspoon grated lemon zest	½	cup granulated sugar
¾	teaspoon ground cinnamon	½	teaspoon salt
¼	teaspoon freshly grated nutmeg	4	tablespoons cold butter, diced
¼	teaspoon ground ginger		

1. Preheat the oven to 375 degrees F. Lightly butter a deep 2-quart baking dish.
2. Combine the pears, brown sugar, lemon juice and zest, ¼ teaspoon of the cinnamon, the nutmeg, and ginger in the baking dish. Spread the pears into an even layer.
3. Combine the flour, oatmeal, nuts, granulated sugar, salt, and the remaining ½ teaspoon cinnamon in a food processor. Pulse the machine on and off a few times to combine roughly.
4. Add the butter to the oatmeal mixture and process until crumbly; do not overprocess.
5. Crumble the oatmeal mixture evenly over the pears and bake in the preheated oven until the top is golden brown and the pears are tender, about 1 hour. Serve warm.

NUTRITION INFORMATION, PER SERVING (¾ CUP): 340 calories, 5 grams protein, 12 grams fat, 60 grams carbohydrates, 250 milligrams sodium, 50 grams cholesterol.

VARIATIONS: Apples, peaches, and nectarines, alone or in combination with fresh berries; nuts, raisins, or dried fruits can be used.

LOWER-FAT VERSION: Cut the butter to 1 or 2 tablespoons, or omit it.

SERVING SUGGESTIONS: If the crisp is made in advance, rewarm it gently in a 275-degree F oven for 15 minutes. French Vanilla Ice Cream (page 172), lightly whipped cream, or wedges or curls of Cheddar or Parmesan cheese are good accompaniments.

Pecan Pie

One of the all-time favorites in diners, cafés, and restaurants across the nation, this Southern classic has stood the test of time. The hallmarks of a good pecan pie are a softly set custard, plenty of sweet pecans, and a well-made crust.

MAKES ONE 9-INCH PIE, 8 SERVINGS

½	recipe Flaky Pie Dough (page 194)	3	eggs, lightly beaten
1½	cups toasted pecans (page 192)	4	tablespoons butter, melted and cooled
½	cup firmly packed light brown sugar	2	teaspoons vanilla extract
2	tablespoons flour	¼	teaspoon salt
¾	cup light corn syrup		

1. Allow the dough to chill in the refrigerator for at least 1 hour or as long as overnight before rolling it out. Preheat the oven to 325 degrees F.
2. Roll out the dough to a thickness of about ¼ inch, and fit it into a 9-inch pie plate. Crimp the edges. Spread the nuts in an even layer over the bottom of the pie.
3. Stir the sugar and flour together in a mixing bowl until well blended.
4. Add the corn syrup, eggs, butter, vanilla, and salt, and blend well.
5. Pour the filling carefully over the nuts, without disturbing them.
6. Bake the pie in the preheated oven for 40 to 45 minutes, or until the center is just set.
7. Cool on a rack for at least 1 hour; serve warm or at room temperature.

NUTRITION INFORMATION, PER SLICE: 380 calories, 4 grams protein, 24 grams fat, 40 grams carbohydrates, 182 milligrams sodium, 117 milligrams cholesterol.

SERVING SUGGESTIONS: Serve the pie warm with French Vanilla Ice Cream (page 172).

To warm the pie before serving, place in a 200-degree F oven for about 20 minutes. Let the pie rest for 10 minutes before slicing and serving. Individual pieces may be warmed in a microwave oven at low power for about 20 seconds.

SHAKER LEMON PIE

*T*his pie was a favorite recipe among the Ohio Shakers. For the best results, be sure to allow the lemons and sugar plenty of time to mellow. Organically grown lemons are best for this, because the rind tends to be less bitter.

MAKES ONE 10-INCH PIE, 10 SERVINGS

4	lemons, sliced paper thin, seeds removed	1	recipe Flaky Pie Dough (page 194)
2⅓	cups sugar	6	eggs

1. Combine the lemon slices and 2 cups of the sugar in a bowl and toss to combine evenly. Cover the bowl and allow the mixture to rest at room temperature for several hours or overnight.

2. Preheat the oven to 450 degrees F. Roll out half the dough into a circle large enough to cover the bottom and sides of a 10-inch tart pan with a removable bottom and fit the dough into the pan.

3. Using a slotted spoon, transfer the lemon slices to the tart pan, allowing as much of the syrup to drain back into the bowl as possible. Sprinkle the remaining ⅓ cup of sugar evenly over the lemon slices.

4. Add 5 eggs to the syrup and beat well; pour the mixture over the lemons.

5. Beat the remaining egg well with 1 tablespoon of water; brush the edge of the bottom crust with some of the mixture.

6. Roll out the remaining dough and cut 3 vents in it. Position it over the tart. Crimp the edges together and brush the top lightly with the remaining egg mixture.

7. Place the tart on a baking sheet and bake it in the preheated oven for 15 minutes. Reduce the temperature to 350 degrees F and continue to bake for another 30 to 40 minutes or until a knife inserted through one of the vents comes out clean.

8. Allow the pie to cool to room temperature before serving or store it in the refrigerator.

NUTRITION INFORMATION, PER SLICE: 535 calories, 7 grams protein, 24 grams fat, 75 grams carbohydrates, 253 milligrams sodium, 127 milligrams cholesterol.

PREPARATION NOTES: Use any remaining scraps of dough to cut out leaves or other decorations for the top of the tart. Use the egg mixture to seal them to the pie, and be sure to brush the mixture over the decorations as well.

The egg mixture, or "wash," should be applied lightly. Do not allow it to form pools in any depressions in the crust.

This pie will retain its quality when stored in the refrigerator for up to 2 days.

SERVING SUGGESTION: This pie would be a wonderful conclusion to a meal built around a roasted or grilled entrée, since it has a refreshing, tart flavor.

Sour Cream and Cinnamon Apple Coffee Cake

*T*his is the coffee cake you might hope to find cooling on a windowsill when you stop to visit a friend after a Saturday morning jog. The type of apple you choose will determine the flavor of the finished cake. Tart apples such as MacIntosh or Granny Smith are fine choices, while Northern Spy or Cortlands will result in a mellower taste.

MAKES 1 CAKE

3 cups flour	¾ cup (1½ sticks) butter, at room temperature
3 teaspoons cinnamon	
2 teaspoons baking powder	1¼ cups sugar
2 teaspoons baking soda	3 eggs
½ teaspoon salt	½ cup sour cream
3 cups peeled, cored, and sliced apples	

1. Preheat the oven to 325 degrees F. Grease and lightly flour a 9-inch-square baking dish.

2. Sift together the flour, 2 teaspoons of the cinnamon, baking powder, baking soda, and salt. Set aside.

3. Finely chop half the apples; set aside the other half.

4. Cream the butter and 1 cup of the sugar until very light and fluffy, 3 to 5 minutes.

5. Add the eggs one at a time, beating well after each addition. Scrape the sides and bottom of the bowl to combine the ingredients thoroughly.

6. Add the chopped apples and sour cream, and stir until combined.

7. Stir in the sifted dry ingredients.

8. Add the sliced apples and fold them into the batter gently, just until they are coated with the batter; take care not to break the slices.

9. Pour the batter into the prepared pan and smooth the top.

10. Stir together the remaining ¼ cup sugar and 1 teaspoon cinnamon, and sprinkle the mixture evenly over the surface of the batter.

11. Bake for 45 minutes to 1 hour in the preheated oven, until a cake tester comes out clean and the edges shrink from the sides of the pan.

NUTRITION INFORMATION, PER 3 X 3-INCH SLICE: 350 calories, 5 grams protein, 16 grams fat, 48 grams carbohydrates, 315 milligrams sodium, 100 milligrams cholesterol.

PREPARATION NOTES: This coffee cake freezes well for up to 3 months. It can be baked in a foil cake pan, cooled, wrapped tightly, and sealed. To serve, thaw the cake at room temperature for an hour, then warm gently in a 250-degree F oven, unwrapped, for about 15 minutes.

SERVING SUGGESTIONS: An excellent addition to a brunch menu. Or serve it as a dessert, warmed and topped with a scoop of French Vanilla Ice Cream (page 172).

ANGEL FOOD SUMMER PUDDING

Summer puddings are made by molding bread or cake slices in bowls or tins and filling them with poached or fresh fruits. They are not cooked, but do resemble traditional steamed puddings in appearance.

MAKES 8 SERVINGS

ANGEL FOOD CAKE:

1	cup cake flour, sifted
1¼	cups sugar
½	teaspoon salt
12	egg whites
2	tablespoons water
1	teaspoon cream of tartar
1	teaspoon vanilla extract

BERRY FILLING:

2	cups stemmed and quartered strawberries
2	cups blackberries
2	cups raspberries
¼	cup sugar
2	tablespoons lemon juice
2	tablespoons Framboise (optional)
1	tablespoon honey, or to taste

1. Preheat the oven to 350 degrees F.

2. Sift the flour, ¼ cup of the sugar, and the salt together twice.

3. Whip the egg whites with the water until foamy; add the cream of tartar and continue to whip until they reach soft peaks.

4. Add the vanilla and, while continuing to whip, gradually add the remaining cup of sugar until all of the sugar is added and the egg whites are glossy and have firm peaks.

5. Gently fold in the sifted flour and sugar mixture. Spoon the batter into an ungreased 9-inch tube pan and bake in the preheated oven until golden brown on top, 40 to 45 minutes.

6. Turn the cake pan upside down onto a baking rack, and let the cake cool completely. Use a metal spatula or thin knife to release the cake from the sides of the pan and unmold it carefully.

7. Combine all the ingredients for the berry filling except the Framboise and honey in a saucepan and simmer over low heat for 15 minutes.

8. Remove the berry mixture from the heat and stir in the Framboise and honey. Use a slotted spoon to lift the berries out of the liquid into a bowl and set them aside.

9. Slice the angel food cake into ½-inch-thick slices. Dip the slices into the berry syrup and turn to coat them evenly.

10. Line eight 1-cup soufflé dishes with plastic wrap large enough to overhang the sides generously. Line the dishes completely with the soaked cake slices and fill the centers with berries. Cover the tops with slices of cake.

11. Fold the plastic wrap over the summer puddings and press down gently. Chill the puddings for at least 3 hours, or overnight.

12. Unmold and unwrap the puddings, and serve with some of the remaining sauce.

NUTRITION INFORMATION, PER SERVING: 285 calories, 7 grams protein, trace of fat, 60 grams carbohydrates, 150 milligrams sodium, 0 milligrams cholesterol.

PREPARATION NOTES: Store-bought angel food cake will give nearly as good results; frozen unsweetened berries can be used if fresh berries are unavailable.

SERVING SUGGESTIONS: Serve with peach ice cream or with cookies and a puff of sweetened whipped cream.

CHOCOLATE BROWNIE CHEESECAKE

*T*his rich and seductive dish combines what probably are the two most popular desserts on anyone's list. The baking temperature is a little lower than it would be for brownies in order to insure that the cheesecake sets gently and stays smooth and creamy.

MAKES ONE 9-INCH CAKE, ABOUT 10 SERVINGS

¾ cup all-purpose flour	¾ cup (1 ½ sticks) unsalted butter, melted and cooled slightly
¾ cup Dutch-process cocoa powder	
½ teaspoon salt	5 eggs
¼ teaspoon baking powder	1 pound cream cheese, at room temperature
¼ teaspoon baking soda	
1⅔ cups granulated sugar	1 teaspoon vanilla extract

1. Preheat the oven to 325 degrees F. Lightly butter and flour a 9-inch springform pan.
2. Sift together the flour, cocoa, salt, baking powder, and baking soda.
3. Combine 1⅓ cups of the sugar and the melted butter in a bowl, and mix thoroughly with a wooden spoon or whisk.
4. Beat 4 eggs together lightly. Add them to the sugar and butter, and mix thoroughly.
5. Fold in the sifted dry ingredients, mixing just long enough to make a smooth batter. Do not overbeat.
6. Pour all but ½ cup of the batter into the prepared pan; reserve the remainder.
7. Beat together the remaining ⅓ cup sugar and the cream cheese by hand or with an electric mixer until very smooth and light.
8. Add the vanilla and the remaining egg to the cream cheese, and mix until well combined.
9. Pour the cream cheese batter into the center of the brownie batter, keeping it away from the sides.
10. With a teaspoon, carefully drop the reserved brownie batter around the top of the cake. Run a table knife through the pools of brownie batter to achieve a marbled effect.
11. Bake for 40 to 50 minutes in the preheated oven. If the top browns too quickly, cover the cake loosely with foil. The cake is done when the edges begin to shrink from the sides of the pan. The center should appear set, but still moist.

NUTRITION INFORMATION, PER SLICE: 400 calories, 8 grams protein, 26 grams fat, 40 grams carbohydrates, 325 milligrams sodium, 180 milligrams cholesterol.

VARIATIONS: Dutch-process cocoa powder has been treated during processing to deepen the color and flavor of the finished dish but any good-quality unsweetened cocoa powder may be used.

Flavor either the brownie or cheesecake batter with up to 2 tablespoons of Kahlua, Amaretto, or Frangelico. Add ½ teaspoon pure almond extract to the cheesecake batter.

SERVING SUGGESTION: There is really nothing more required to accompany this dessert than a cup of coffee made from dark-roasted beans.

BERRY COBBLER

*C*obblers are favorite home-style desserts that vary from region to region. In the South, cobblers are topped with a biscuit-style crust, but this one has a delicious cake on top.

SERVES 8

1½	cups cake flour or all-purpose flour	1	cup sugar
2	teaspoons baking soda	1	egg, lightly beaten
1	teaspoon cream of tartar	½	cup buttermilk
1	teaspoon salt	3	pints berries, preferably raspberries,
½	cup butter, softened		blackberries, or blueberries

1. Grease a 9 x 13-inch baking dish. Preheat the oven to 350 degrees F.

2. Sift together the flour, baking soda, cream of tarter, and salt.

3. In a large mixing bowl, cream the butter and ¾ cup of the sugar until very light. Beat in the egg.

4. Add the flour to the butter mixture alternately with the buttermilk, beginning and ending with the flour mixture. Blend to incorporate.

5. Arrange the berries in the baking dish. Scatter the remaining ¼ cup sugar over the berries. Spoon the batter over the berries.

6. Bake for 40 to 50 minutes in the preheated oven until the crust is golden brown and a toothpick inserted into the top comes out clean. Serve warm.

NUTRITION INFORMATION, PER 3-INCH-SQUARE SERVING: 335 calories, 45 grams protein, 13 grams fat, 53 grams carbohydrates, 600 milligrams sodium, 65 milligrams cholesterol.

SERVING SUGGESTIONS: This cobbler is wonderful served warm with ice cream, whipped cream, or just a pool of heavy cream.

AMERICAN BOUNTY FUDGE CAKE

*F*udge is an American-born confection that originated in women's colleges such as Vassar, Radcliffe, and Wellesley around the 1900s. This cake has a dense fudgy texture and an intense chocolate flavor.

MAKES ONE 10-INCH CAKE, 16 SERVINGS

1¼	pounds semisweet chocolate	½	cup sugar
1½	cups all-purpose flour	3	tablespoons corn oil
½	cup cocoa powder	6	eggs, lightly beaten
½	teaspoon salt	1½	tablespoons vanilla extract
1½	cups butter, softened	¼	cup corn syrup

1. Lightly grease a 10-inch cake pan. Preheat the oven to 375 degrees F. Melt the chocolate in the top of a double boiler or in a microwave oven; set aside to cool.

2. Sift together the flour, cocoa powder, and salt.

3. Cream the butter and sugar together in the bowl of an electric mixer until very light and fluffy. Add the oil and mix, scraping the sides and bottom of the bowl as necessary, about 2 minutes, until very smooth.

4. Add the eggs and continue to beat, scraping the sides of the bowl as needed, until the mixture is very light and fluffy.

5. Add the vanilla and corn syrup, and continue mixing until very smooth, about 3 more minutes.

6. Stir in the melted chocolate until thoroughly blended.

7. Fold the sifted dry ingredients into the batter in three stages, making sure that each addition is thoroughly incorporated before adding the next.

8. Pour the batter into the prepared pan and bake in the preheated oven for about 30 minutes or until a skewer inserted ½ inch from the edge comes out clean; the center should remain soft and fudgy.

9. Cool the cake completely on a rack before removing from the pan.

NUTRITION INFORMATION, PER SLICE: 470 calories, 5 grams protein, 34 grams fat, 40 grams carbohydrates, 303 milligrams sodium, 148 milligrams cholesterol.

PREPARATION NOTES: This cake holds well under refrigeration or in the freezer. Allow individual slices to return to room temperature or warm them briefly on the lowest power setting in a microwave oven before serving.

VARIATIONS: Add a generous cup of toasted nuts (page 192) to the batter before baking. Walnuts and pecans are perennial favorites, but try hazelnuts, almonds, or cashews for an elegant twist.

SERVING SUGGESTIONS: A puff of unsweetened whipped cream is the only embellishment this cake requires. Serve or follow with rich espresso coffee.

GINGERCAKE

Sweet, fragrant, and spicy, this cake is delicious at breakfast or afternoon tea.

MAKES ONE 9-INCH CAKE

1½	cups all-purpose flour		1	cup sugar
2	teaspoons ground ginger		½	cup molasses
1	teaspoon baking powder		½	cup buttermilk
½	teaspoon baking soda		2	eggs
1	teaspoon salt			Confectioners' sugar (optional)
½	cup unsalted butter			

1. Grease a 9-inch baking pan. Preheat the oven to 350 degrees F.

2. Sift together the flour, ginger, baking powder, baking soda, and salt.

3. Cream together the butter and sugar until very light. Add the molasses and buttermilk and continue beating until the mixture is quite smooth.

4. Add the eggs one at a time, beating until blended after each addition.

5. Add the sifted dry ingredients and stir until the batter is very smooth.

6. Spread the batter into the prepared pan and bake for 35 minutes, or until the center springs back when lightly pressed with a fingertip and the edges have shrunk away from the pan.

7. Cool the cake thoroughly before unmolding from the pan. Dust with confectioners' sugar and cut into squares. Serve with sweetened cream or lemon curd.

NUTRITION INFORMATION, PER 3-INCH-SQUARE SERVING: 315 calories, 4 grams protein, 12 grams fat, 49 grams carbohydrates, 350 milligrams sodium, 75 milligrams cholesterol.

INGREDIENTS

The recipes in this book were prepared and tested using:
- Choice grade meats
- Grade AA unsalted butter
- Eggs graded "Large"
- All-purpose flour, except where indicated
- Table salt
- Fresh herbs, except where dried versions are specifically indicated
- Whole milk
- Vegetable oil, such as corn oil, canola, or olive, peanut, sunflower, except where particular oils are indicated, such as extra-virgin olive oil

METHODS

Dried Beans

Most beans, with the exception of lentils and black-eyed peas, should be soaked in cool water for several hours or overnight before cooking.

A faster method is to place the beans in a pot and cover them with cool water. Bring the water to a boil, then remove the pot from the heat. Cover and set aside for 1 hour. Drain the beans, and continue with the recipe.

Peeling and Seeding Fresh Tomatoes

To peel fresh tomatoes, bring a pot of water to a rolling boil. Score an X in the bottom of each tomato with the tip of a sharp paring knife, then lower into the boiling water for 30 to 45 seconds. Remove with a slotted spoon and place in a bowl of cold or ice water to stop the cooking. When the tomatoes are cool, pull away the skin, cut the tomato in half and squeeze out the seeds.

Plumping Dried Fruits and Vegetables

To plump dried ingredients such as mushrooms, tomatoes, or fruits, cover with boiling water and let rest for at least 15 minutes. Drain them and reserve the liquid for use in another dish such as a stew, soup, or broth. If the liquid appears cloudy, strain it through a coffee filter or fine sieve.

Dried fruits can also be plumped in a little cognac, port, or wine for up to an hour. The soaking liquid is generally included in the recipe for additional flavor.

Roasting and Peeling Peppers

Hold a whole pepper in the flame of a gas burner with tongs or a kitchen fork, turning the pepper until all of its sides are blackened, *or*

Cut the peppers in half, pull away the seeds, and rub the outsides lightly with oil. Place them, cut side down, on a baking sheet and broil until blackened.

Once the peppers are blackened, place them in a plastic bag, close tightly, and let them rest until they are cool enough to handle. Pull away the charred skin, using a paring knife as necessary. Discard the seeds, ribs, and stems.

When working with very hot chiles, it is advisable to wear plastic or latex gloves to protect the skin.

Toasting and Chopping Nuts, Seeds, and Whole Spices

Toast small quantities in a dry sauté pan or skillet over medium-high heat until a rich aroma is apparent. Transfer to a plate to cool before chopping or grinding.

Toast larger quantities in a 400-degree F oven for 5 to 10 minutes. Spread the nuts, seeds, or spices in a single layer on a baking sheet. Stir once or twice during toasting to brown evenly. Remove from the baking sheet immediately to avoid overcooking or burning.

Once the nuts, seeds, or spices are cooled to room temperature, they can be chopped or ground as needed. Chop nuts by hand using a chef's knife, or place them in a mini-food processor and pulse it on and off just until they are coarsely chopped. Seeds and spices can be ground in a mortar and pestle, coffee or spice grinder, or a blender.

Cleaning Mushrooms

Most mushrooms are cleaned by wiping the caps and stems with a piece of paper towel, a soft cloth, or a soft brush. However, if they are extremely dirty, they can be rinsed in cool water. Drain thoroughly in a colander or wipe dry before slicing or chopping.

The stems of wild and domestic mushrooms can be trimmed as necessary and may be included in most preparations. Shiitakes are an exception; their tough stems are generally cut away before cooking.

RECIPES

Vegetable Broth

This stock can be used in place of water or chicken broth in grain or bean dishes, in soups and stews, or for steaming vegetables. Other vegetables that will not give the finished stock a strong odor or color, such as beets and beet greens, can be added or substituted for the ones here. Starchy vegetables may make the stock foam over as it simmers.

MAKES ABOUT 2 QUARTS

2	teaspoons olive or corn oil
1 to 2	garlic cloves, finely minced
2	teaspoons minced shallots
2	quarts water
½	cup dry white wine or vermouth (optional)
1	large onion, thinly sliced
1	leek, trimmed and sliced
1	stalk celery, thinly sliced on the bias
1	carrot, thinly sliced
1	parsnip, thinly sliced
1	cup broccoli stems, thinly sliced
1	cup sliced fennel (with some tops)
4 to 5	whole black peppercorns
½	teaspoon juniper berries
1	bay leaf
1	sprig fresh thyme, or ¼ teaspoon dried leaves

1. Heat the olive oil in a large pot over medium heat. Add the garlic and shallots, and sauté, stirring frequently, until they are translucent, 3 to 4 minutes.

2. Add the remaining ingredients, and bring the broth slowly just to a boil over medium heat; reduce the heat to low.

3. Simmer the stock for 30 to 40 minutes, or until it has a good, rich flavor.

4. Strain the stock through a sieve and cool completely before storing it in the refrigerator for up to 4 days, or in a freezer for up to 2 months.

NUTRITION INFORMATION, PER CUP: 14 calories, 1 gram protein, trace of fat, 2 grams carbohydrates, 10 milligrams sodium, 0 milligrams cholesterol.

Fish Broth

The fish bones must be perfectly fresh; freeze them if the broth is not to be made immediately. Shells from shrimp, crab, and lobsters can also be used, and similarly stored in the freezer if necessary.

MAKES ABOUT 1 QUART

1	tablespoon vegetable oil
2½	pounds fish bones and/or shells
1	onion, thinly sliced
1	leek, trimmed and thinly sliced
1	stalk celery, trimmed and thinly sliced
½	cup mushrooms or mushroom stems, thinly sliced (optional)
½	cup dry white wine (optional)
5	cups cold water
1	sprig fresh thyme, tarragon, or dill
2 to 3	stems parsley
1	bay leaf
3 to 4	whole black peppercorns

1. Heat the oil in a saucepan. Add the fish-bones and/or shells, onions, leeks, celery, and mushrooms. Stir until all ingredients are evenly coated with oil. Cover the pot and cook, without stirring, over low heat for about 5 minutes.
2. Add the wine, and simmer until the wine is reduced by half. Then add the water and the remaining ingredients. Bring the broth just to a simmer. Continue to simmer over low heat for 35 to 45 minutes.
3. Strain the broth through a sieve. Discard the bones, vegetables, and herbs. If the broth is not to be used right away, cool it thoroughly before storing it in the refrigerator for up to 3 days or in the freezer for 4 to 6 weeks. Bring the broth to a boil and check it for spoilage before using.

This broth can be used to prepare risotto or pilafs of various grains which can be garnished or served with seafood dishes. It also can be used as the basis for fish stews like cioppino.

NUTRITION INFORMATION, PER CUP: 20 calories, 4 grams protein, 1 gram fat, 1 gram carbohydrates, 10 milligrams sodium, trace of cholesterol.

Chicken Broth

MAKES ABOUT 2 QUARTS

4	pounds chicken bones
3	quarts cold water
1	large onion, thinly sliced
1	carrot, thinly sliced
1	stalk celery, thinly sliced
5 to 6	whole black peppercorns
3 to 4	parsley stems
1	bay leaf
1	sprig fresh thyme

1. Place the chicken bones in a large pot with enough cold water to cover them by 2 inches. Bring the water to a boil over medium heat.
2. As the water comes to a boil, skim any foam that rises to the surface. Adjust the heat to maintain a slow, lazy simmer.
3. When the broth has simmered for 1½ to 2 hours, add the remaining ingredients. Continue to simmer, skimming the surface as necessary, for another hour.
4. Strain the broth and let it cool to room temperature; store in the refrigerator for up to 5 days, or in the freezer for up to 3 months.

To remove fat from the broth, cool it thoroughly in the refrigerator. The fat will come to the surface and harden and will then be easy to lift off.

NUTRITION INFORMATION, PER CUP: 20 calories, 2 grams protein, trace of fat, 1 gram carbohydrates, 10 milligrams sodium, 1 milligram cholesterol.

Flaky Pie Dough

FOR ONE DOUBLE- OR 2 SINGLE-CRUST PIES

2⅔	cups all-purpose flour
1	teaspoon salt
1	cup cold shortening
½	cup very cold water

1. Stir the flour and salt together with a fork to blend well.

2. Cut the shortening into the flour using a fork, a pastry cutter, or two knives until the mixture looks like extremely coarse meal. There should be some clumps of shortening that are about the size of a pea.

3. Make a well in the center of the flour-shortening mixture. Add the cold water and quickly stir together into a shaggy mass with a fork. Do not overwork the dough.

4. Turn the dough out onto a lightly floured work surface. Knead once or twice, just until the dough forms a ball. Divide the dough into two roughly equal pieces; pat each piece into an even disk, wrap well, and chill in the refrigerator for at least 1 hour.

5. Unwrap one piece of the dough at a time. Place it on a floured work surface. Scatter a little extra flour over the top of the dough and roll it out into an even circle. It should be about 2 inches wider in diameter than your pie plate. Fold the dough in half, and gently lift it into the pan.

6. Settle the dough into the pan, pressing it, without pulling, gently against the sides and bottom. Trim away any excess overhang.

FOR A DOUBLE-CRUST PIE: Add the filling at this point, according to recipe directions. Roll out the second piece of dough as directed above, cut vents, and lay it over the filling. Seal and crimp the edges.

FOR A SINGLE-CRUST PIE: Trim away any excess overhang. Crimp the edges, fill the pie, and bake as directed.

TO BAKE BLIND: Prick the dough evenly over the bottom and sides. Line the dough with a piece of waxed or parchment paper and fill with dry beans or pie weights. Bake at 400 degrees F just until the edges of the dough appear dry, but have not taken on any color, 6 to 7 minutes. Remove the beans and paper, return the pie shell to the oven, and bake an additional 5 minutes, or until the bottom of the crust appears dry as well.

FREEZING PIE DOUGH: Roll out dough and fit it into an aluminum pie plate. Crimp the edges, as you would normally, wrap in foil or plastic wrap, then store in the freezer for up to 2 months.

Index